ARTIST ARCHIVES™ INTRODUCTION BY MAX ALLAN COLLINS

EXOTIC LADIES

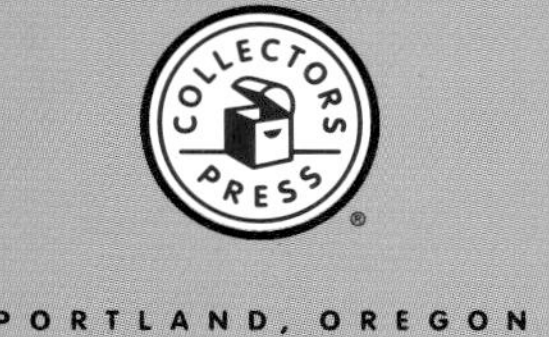

PORTLAND, OREGON

EXOTIC

LADIES

INTRODUCTION

Design Principia Graphica
Technical Assistance Hoover H.Y. Li
Editor Ann Granning Bennett

The publisher would like to extend a special thanks to Dean Patzer and LeRoy Darwin for supplying various images in this book.

Distributed to the U.S. Book Trade by *Universe Publishing*, a division of Rizzoli International Publications, Inc. through St. Martin's Press, 175 Fifth Avenue, New York, New York 10010

Distributed in Canada by *McClelland & Stewart*
Printed in Hong Kong

Library of Congress Cataloging-in-Publication Data
Collins, Max Allan.
Exotic ladies / Max Allan Collins. — 1st American ed.
p. cm. — (Artist archives)
ISBN 1-888054-36-0 (pbk. : alk. paper)
1. Erotic art — United States. 2. Women in art 3. Calendar art — United States. I. Title. II. Series.
N8217.E6C66 1999
769'.424—dc21 99-29641
CIP

First American Edition

9 8 7 6 5 4 3 2 1

FOR A FREE CATALOG WRITE TO COLLECTORS PRESS, INC.

P.O. Box 230986
Portland, Oregon 97281
Toll Free 800-423-1848
Or visit our website at *www.collectorspress.com*

BEFORE THE CALENDAR GIRL settled into swimwear and other provocative but contemporary attire, the artists depicting these fantasy visions of female perfection frequently chose to cloak their subjects in the gauzy eroticism of a mythic past. Helens of Troy, Salomes, Cleopatras, and American-Indian maidens perched, posed, and pranced across the pages of calendars across America, their scanty attire and unabashed eroticism made acceptable, even proper, by the patina of history. Vaguely artistic in their jeweled brassières, elaborate headdresses, and sheer sarongs, these sirens seem to have slipped through a loophole in the prudish American contract.

This was the same loophole the vixens of Hollywood's Biblical epics slithered and slinked through — famed director Cecil B. De Mille constantly slipped scantily clad (and sometimes unclad) beauties past the censors in the guise of history and Bible lessons. Even today, Claudette Colbert's nude milk bath in "Sign of the Cross" (1932) is shockingly sexy. Early 1930s talkie stars like Colbert and silent "vamps" like Theda Bara wore exotic, revealing attire that no doubt inspired many of the artists in this book.

All of the images here — whether by famous artists or unknown ones — echo the Hollywood influence. "The Spirit of the Nile" by G.C. Orde might well be called "The Spirit of Cecil B. De Mille." Faces in these pages recall forgotten stars like Bara, Colbert, Mary Fickford, and Clara Bow.

Easily the most famous of the artists represented here, Rolf Armstrong has been called the "father" of the pin-up. Indeed, he enjoyed a career of creating glamour-girl images that began in 1919, thriving well into the 1950s. Though modern subject matter was a constant throughout his career — his 1940s and 1950s beauties are often bikinied — Armstrong excelled at exoticism. His specialty was Spanish attire, with Carmen-like subjects draped in lace and crowned by over-sized sombreros.

Armstrong (1889–1960) came to fame in the 1920s, an era his romantic, drowsily sensual females seem to typify. Armstrong's expert, confident use of the pastel medium spawned such famous followers as Billy DeVorss, Earl Moran, and Zoë Mozert, and his approach itself (if not his favored medium) was a clear influence on such fellow pin-up artists as Alberto Vargas, Enoch Bolles, and Merlin Enabnit.

Armstrong illustrated many magazines and song sheet covers (all highly collectible now). He was perhaps best known for his close-up portraits of dreamily sensuous Clara Bow-ish "It" girls, who seemed to emerge from a brilliant swirl of some single vivid color — often red, and in exotic subjects, blue — and his nonspecific backgrounds from which a specific girl emanated became a convention followed by countless others.

The popularity of his sultry close-ups aside, it was the artist's dazzlingly smiling, flowingly maned, supple-limbed calendar girls for Brown & Bigelow that set the glamour-art standard. Michigan-born Armstrong, who studied at the famed Chicago Art Institute, contributed covers to periodicals such as *College Humor*, *Life*, and *Shrine* magazine; his advertising accounts included Oneida Silversmiths.

With a pastel palate of 3,600 colors, Armstrong worked from live models in his Manhattan studio, creating enormous originals (typical size: 28" by 39"!). A one-time pro boxer and devoted seaman, ruggedly handsome Armstrong was rarely seen without his yachting cap, and he enjoyed promoting both a man's man persona and (in numerous photo layouts) living the fantasy life of an artist surrounded by beautiful models.

"The Enchantress" (seen in this volume) is a fine example of Armstrong at his lush, seductively romantic best. The dark-haired beauty is at once timeless and a Clara Bow flapper. Her shapely nearly nude figure extends like a bold exclamation point below the circular, art-deco element of the massive tray she is rather incongruously bearing. Again, the dominance of a single color — the blue background echoed by the engraving of the tray — is typical Armstrong technique.

The other Armstrong image in this book — "Cleopatra" — is less typical. The circular design elements of window and shield intermingle with the sinuous splash of orange-red echoing the slinky yet voluptuous (and improbably blonde) Queen of the Nile, representing a not uncommon interweaving by the artist of art deco and art nouveau.

Armstrong's influence was felt by every other artist represented in this volume. "Alluring" by M. Bron, for example, includes both the blue backdrop and the characteristic Armstrong circular design element (though the exquisitely detailed painting casts its own special spell). But no other illustrator was more under Armstrong's sway than Billy DeVorss, who some have understandably dismissed as a shameless imitator.

A native of St Joseph, Missouri, DeVorss worked out of New York's Greenwich Village from the mid-1930s until returning to the midwest in the early 1950s. The grip Armstrong held on DeVorss even extended to DeVorss' excessive flourish of a signature. Working like his idol, the largely self-schooled DeVorss customarily painted in pastels, from live models, creating calendar girls who usually displayed exaggerated dazzling smiles and shapely long-limbed forms in the Armstrong manner.

Nonetheless, DeVorss has his own unique charm — his works, while inconsistent, have a glow, a warmth, his girls-next-door radiating a good-natured sexuality. And, as I have noted elsewhere, while Armstrong conveyed glamour, DeVorss' favorite subject was romance (his favorite model, his wife).

While most of the images in this collection are from the 1920s, the DeVorss examples are from the 1930s to the 1940s — reflecting the artist's position as a follower of Armstrong. "A Sheer Beauty" calendar pose herein, with its circular yellow design element, shows how slavish an imitator of Armstrong DeVorss could be. "The Loveliest Jewel of All," another unabashed though lovely imitation of Armstrong in his exotic mode, may have seemed quite out-of-date at the time of its publication. (Note the bee-stung lips of the blonde temptress.) His "A Dancing Darling" denotes the movement from exotic subject matter to exotic dancing — this pin-up is more likely a stripper than a Babylonian princess. If she is more satisfying than the other two more overtly exotic poses, that only reflects DeVorss' own overriding interest in the All-American Girl.

Among the lesser known (and even anonymous) contributors this collection are several prominent names in illustration.

Hy Hintermeister was actually a father-and-son team, John (born in 1870 in Switzerland, where he received his art education at the Zurich Museum Art School) and Henry (born in 1897 in New York, where he received his art education at Pratt Institute). The Hintermeisters were versatile, skillful journeymen illustrators who trod much the same path as Norman Rockwell, without receiving his enduring household fame.

Still, like Rockwell, "Hy Hintermeister" was a storyteller, and he specialized in the same sort of warm, folksy humor on scores of magazine covers and calendars. Small-town life — often centering on children, little boys reeling in fish, little girls "helping" traffic cops, grandmas and grandpas interacting comically with their grandkids — was the team's prime subject matter.

But, in between kids and codgers, the father and son created their fair share of "Salomes, hula girls, and bright young women" as Rick and Charlotte Martin described the team's subjects in *Vintage Illustration*. "Egyptian Splendor" is a typically overripe calendar image of the genre, with its nearly nude subject, splendidly arrayed in a blue-and-gold world right out of Maxfield Parrish — complete with a sphinx looking on!

The sunny goodness of youth radiates from the girls created by gifted Gene Pressler. Even his most exotic beauties have a hint of the girl-next-door, and his work foreshadows the approach and subject matter of the artists who followed him into the 1940s and 1950s — a journey Pressler himself, sadly, did not make.

Born in Jersey City, New Jersey, in 1894, Pressler made a significant mark in commercial illustration prior to his tragic early demise at age 39. His Pompeian Beauty Cream ads — tall, narrow calendar-girl images — brought him fame and more upper-echelon advertising accounts. While Maxfield Parrish was gaining attention for his General Electric/Edison Mazda light ads, the Westinghouse Company chose Pressler for a similar, rival campaign; and Pressler was in demand as an artist for jigsaw puzzles at the early 1930s peak of that craze.

A master of pastels whose lighting effects remain much admired, Pressler was heavily swayed by the standard of beauty suggested by silent movie stars such as Bow, Pola Negri, and Mary Pickford. His exotic images frequently appear to have a modern setting — like the exquisite flapper trying on costumes from an attic trunk in "Jewels." The wealth of detail in this particular pastel painting reveals an extraordinarily proficient level of craftsmanship.

His "Sweet Rose of Araby" might well be a flapper at a costume ball, and the rosy-cheeked, coyly peering princess of "Where Unimagined Beauty Dwells" might well be on the set of a film. These are modern girls, for the most part innocent ones, and the aficionado of calendar girls can only wonder — with some bittersweet longing — what heartbreaking beauties young Pressler might have conjured up had he not been taken from us by a bout of pneumonia.

Among other artists under Armstrong's spell were Irene Patten and her sister Laurette. (Pin-up experts Charles G. Martignette and Louis K. Meisel, in their sumptuous survey, *The Great American Pin-Up*, speculate that the sisters worked together.) Creating hundreds of pretty-girl images for various calendar companies out of their Chicago, Illinois, studio, the Patten sisters worked in Armstrong's medium — pastel — on similarly large canvases.

The subjects of the Patten pastels are glowing, apple-cheeked girls, sometimes echoing Hollywood stars such as Jean Harlow and Joan Crawford, often in modern settings, striking young women in gowns, nude nymphs at poolsides and, of course, the occasional exotic goddess. As with DeVorss and Pressler, Patten seems to be portraying modern girls playing dress up. The stunningly beautiful, exceptionally well-rendered "Lady in Red" has more sophistication than the average Patten girl; but in all her poise and elegance, she remains a modern woman (that is, circa 1930), at odds with the quaint loveliness of her fringed, boldly topless outfit.

Similarly, the unknown artist of "A Lily of the Valley" also drapes a lovely contemporary female in exotic attire and surroundings. The conceit that these Betty Boops of the 1920s and early 1930s are wrapped up in the ostentatious trappings of ancient days (we're talking Hollywood antiquity here) makes the calendar girls of this collection all the sweeter. They remain as pretty, as shapely, as desirable as ever — qualities only amplified by the nostalgic frisson of two yesterdays colliding.

These exotic ladies are ever now as their artists intended them to be . . . timeless treasures.

Sources: *The Great American Pin-Up*, Charles G. Martignette and Louis K. Meisel, Taschen, 1996; *Vintage Illustration*, Rick and Charlotte Martin, Collectors Press, Inc., 1997.

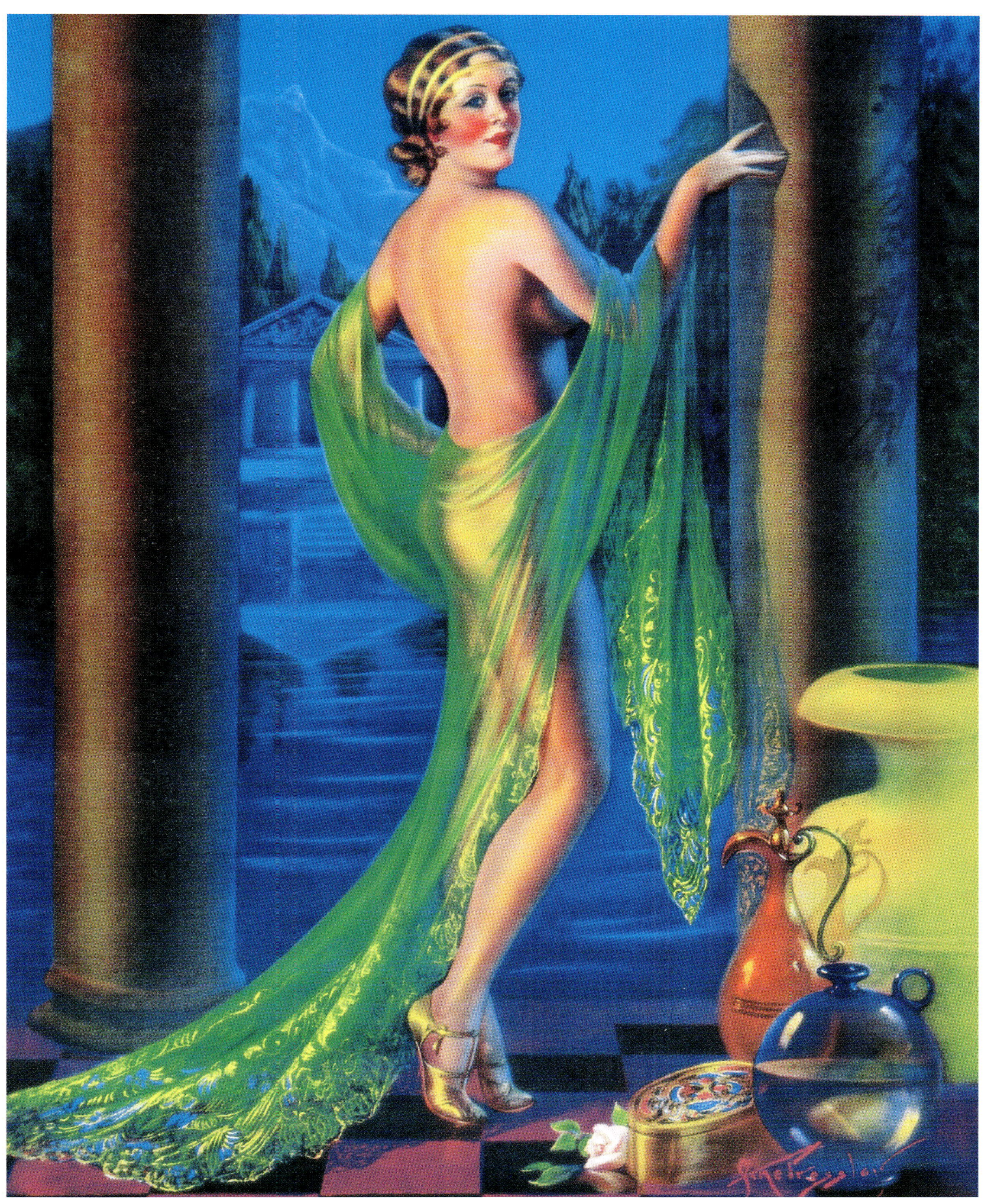

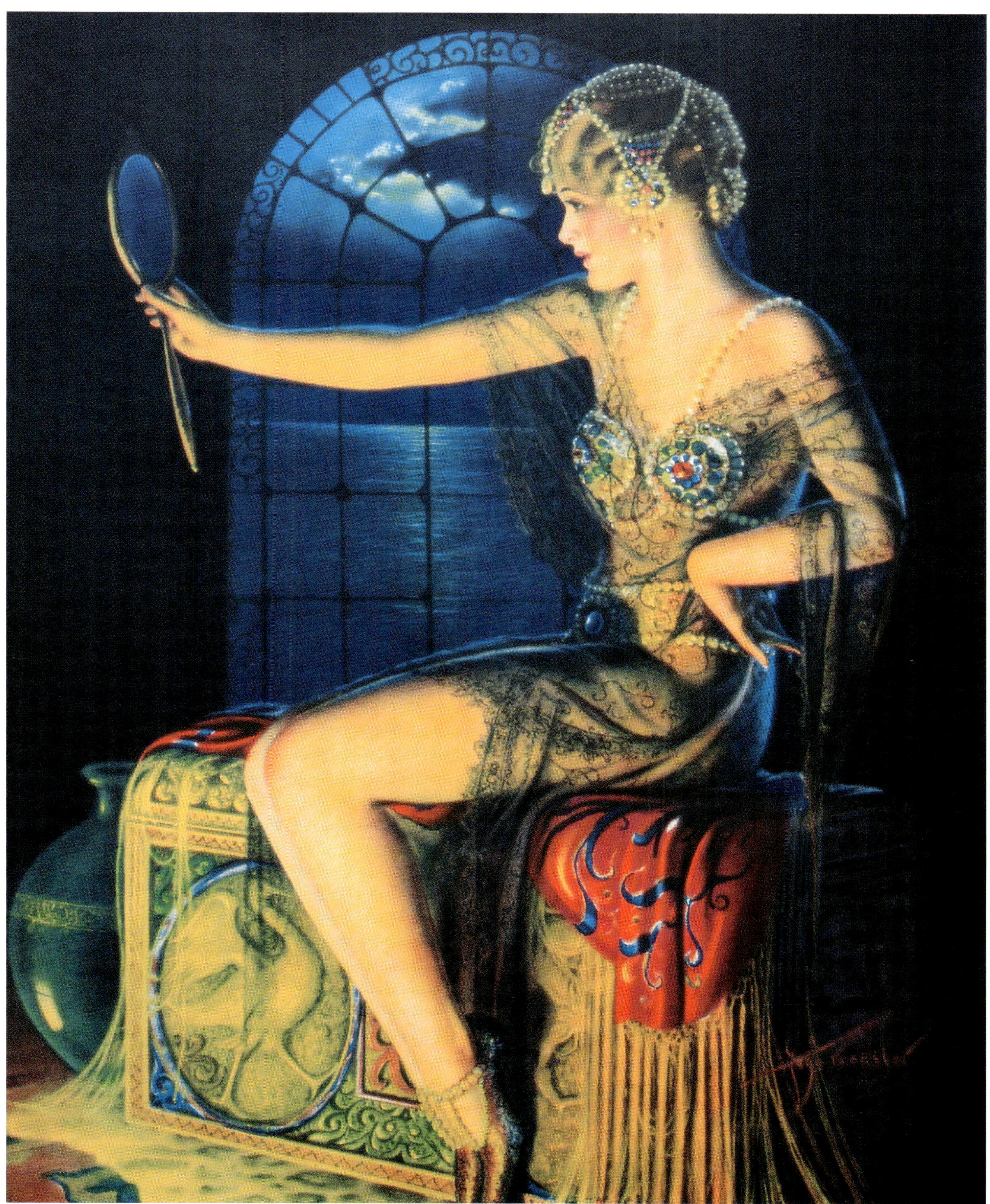

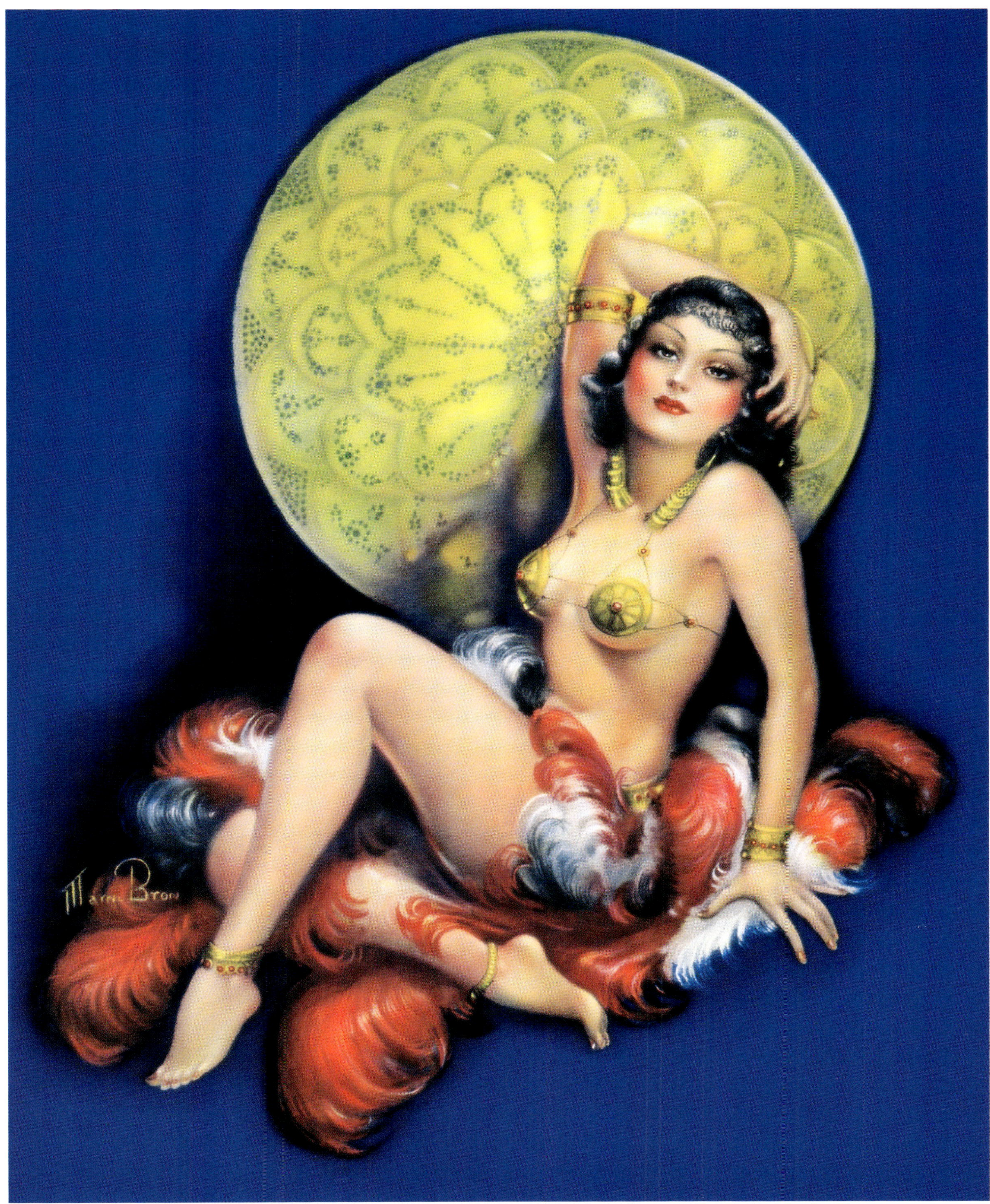

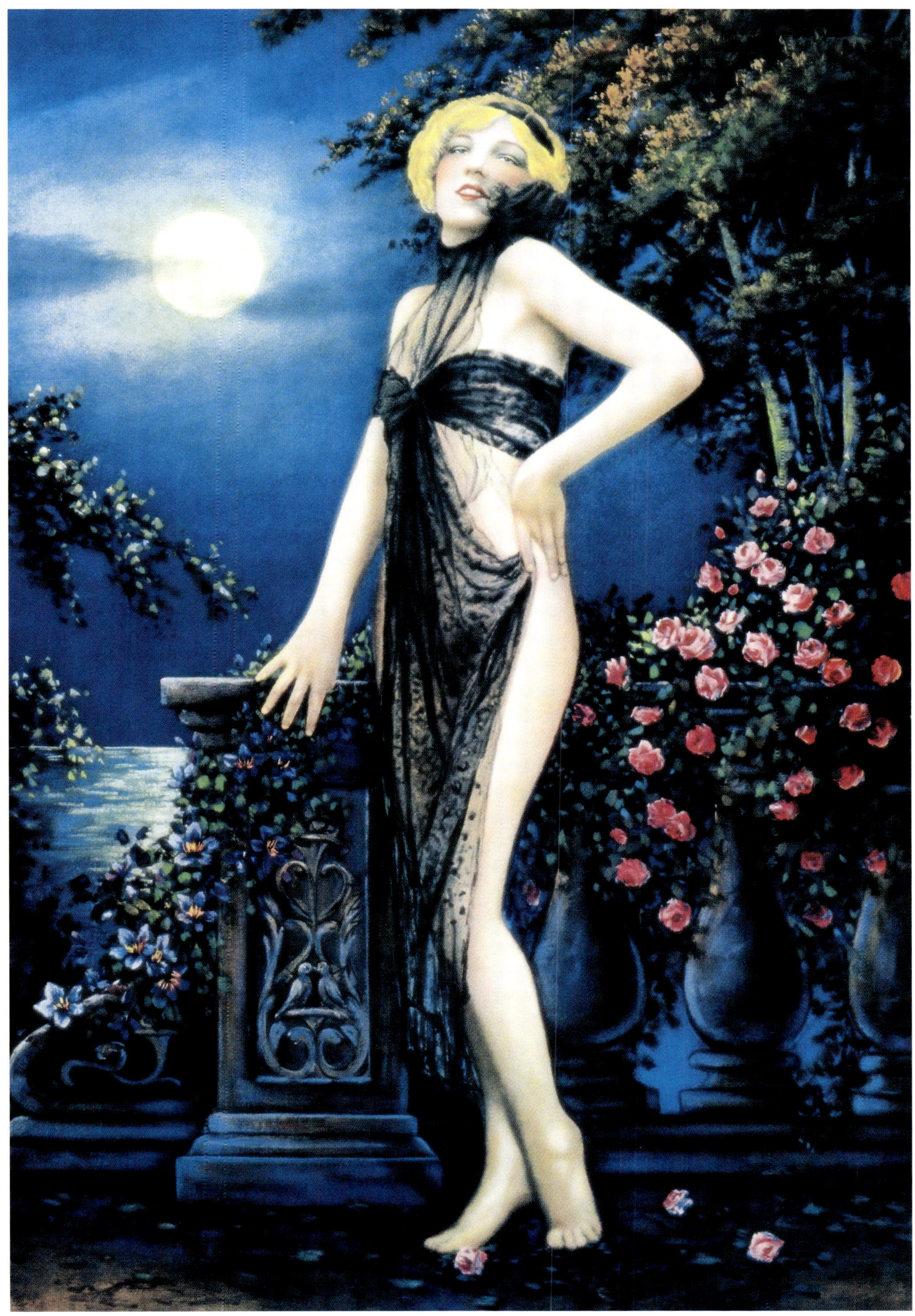

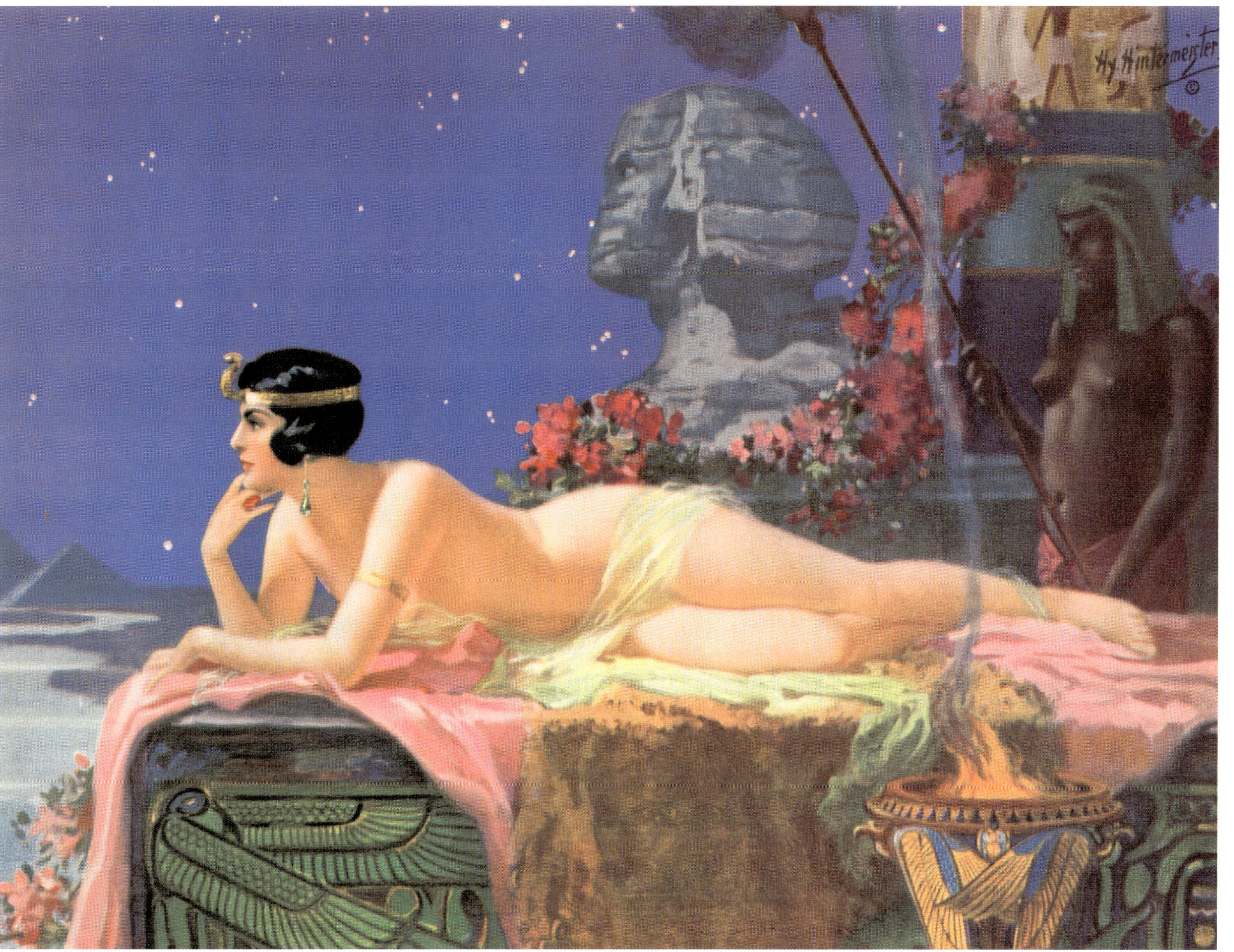
Hy Hintermeister ©

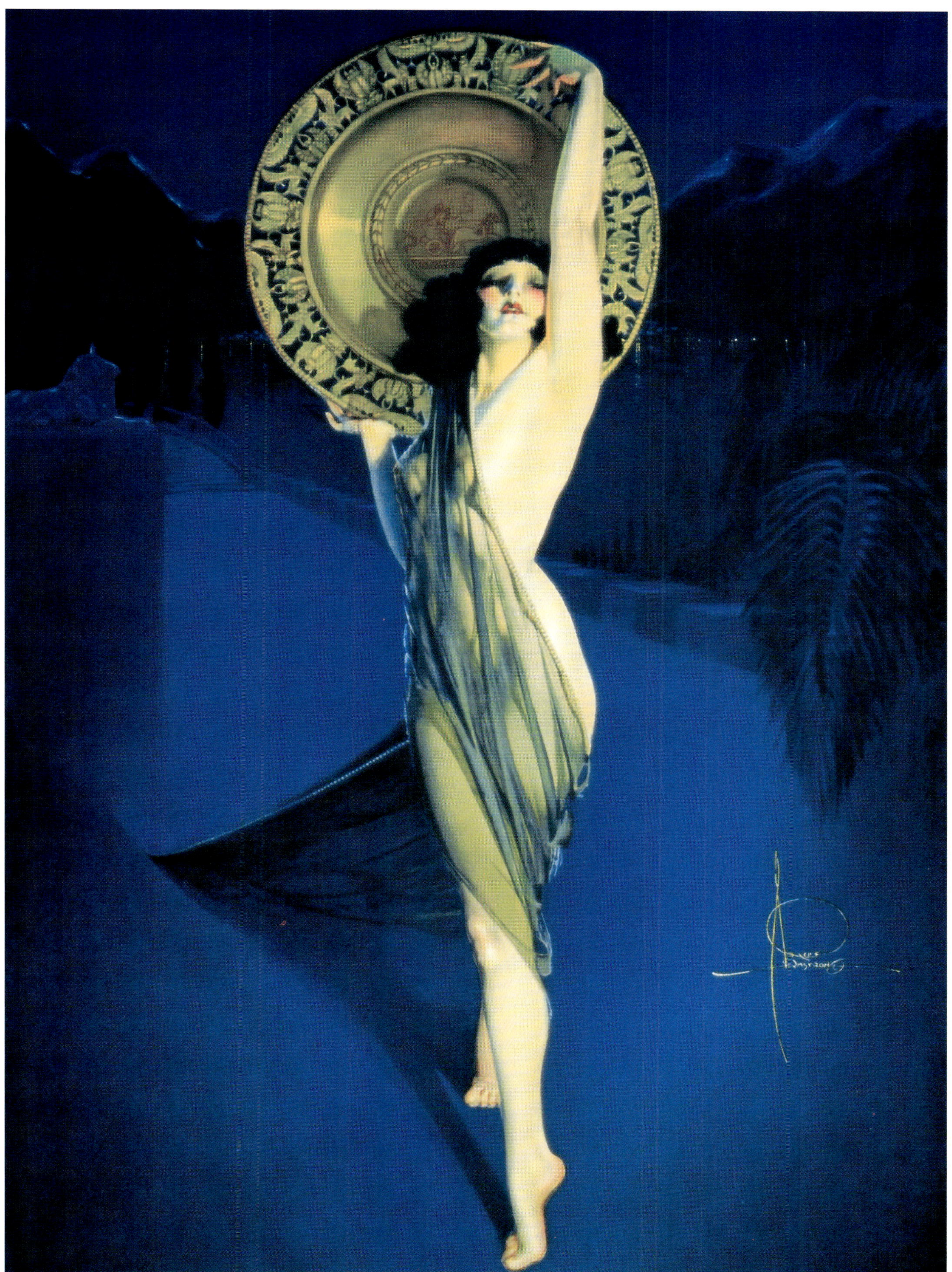

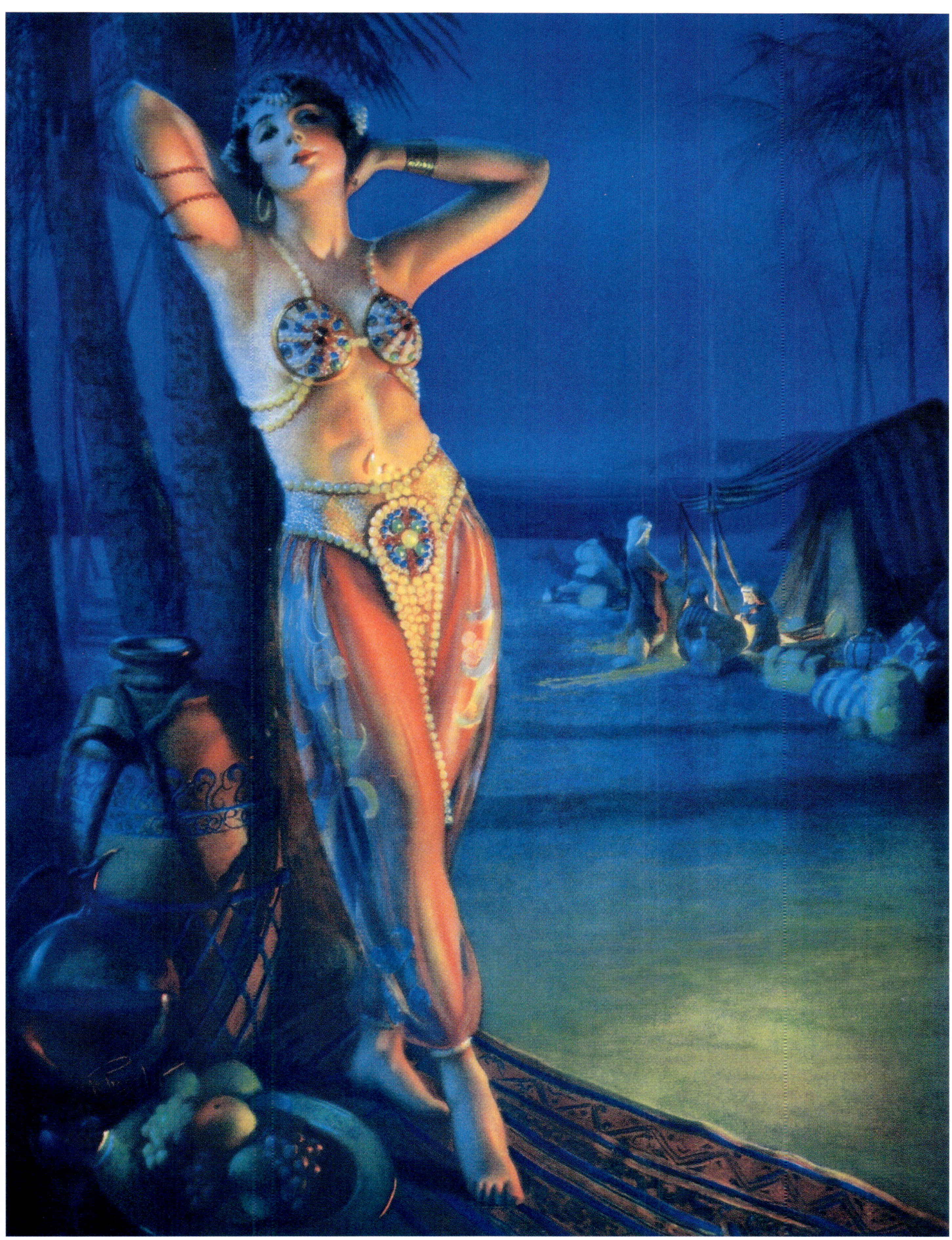

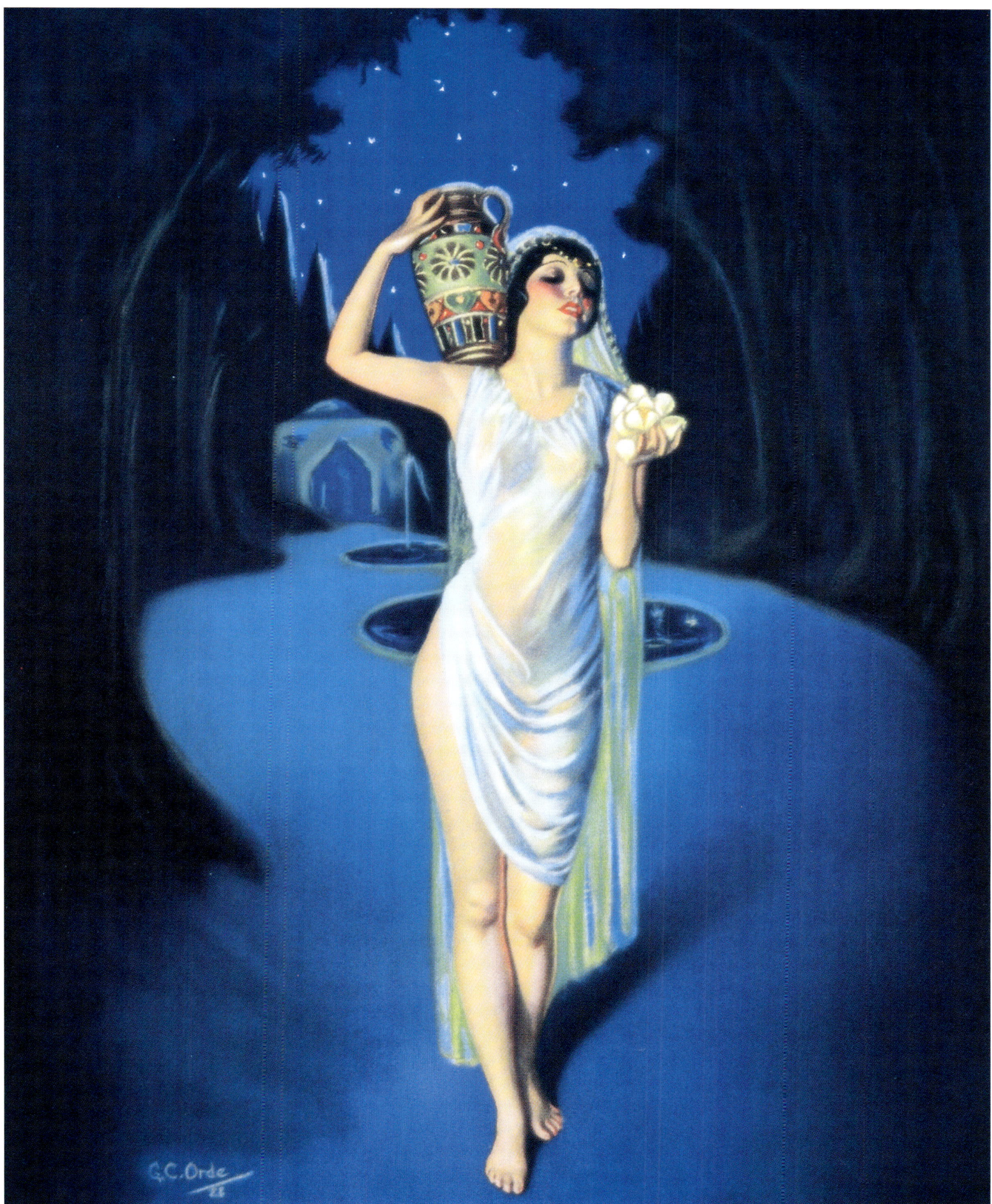
G.C. Orde
28

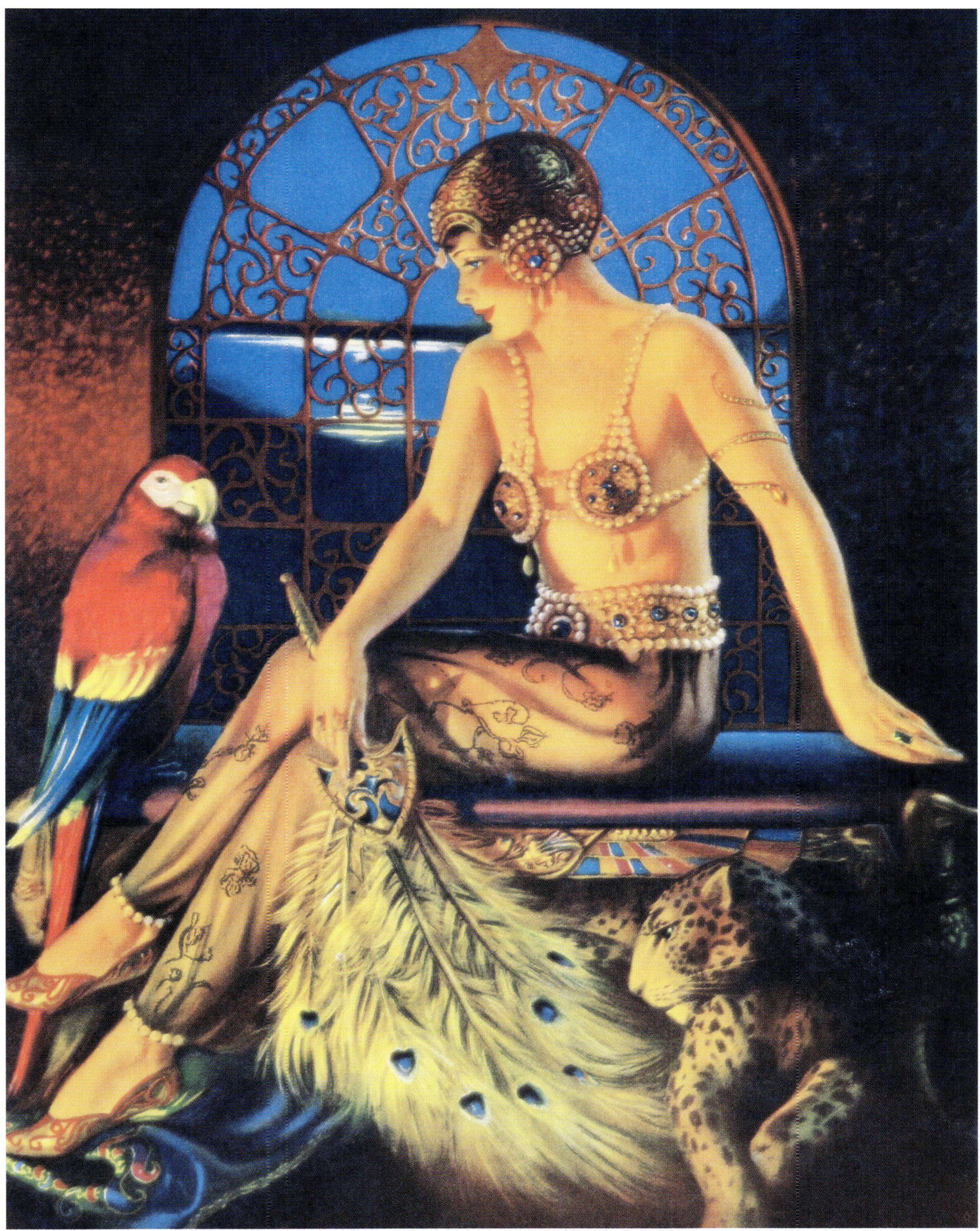

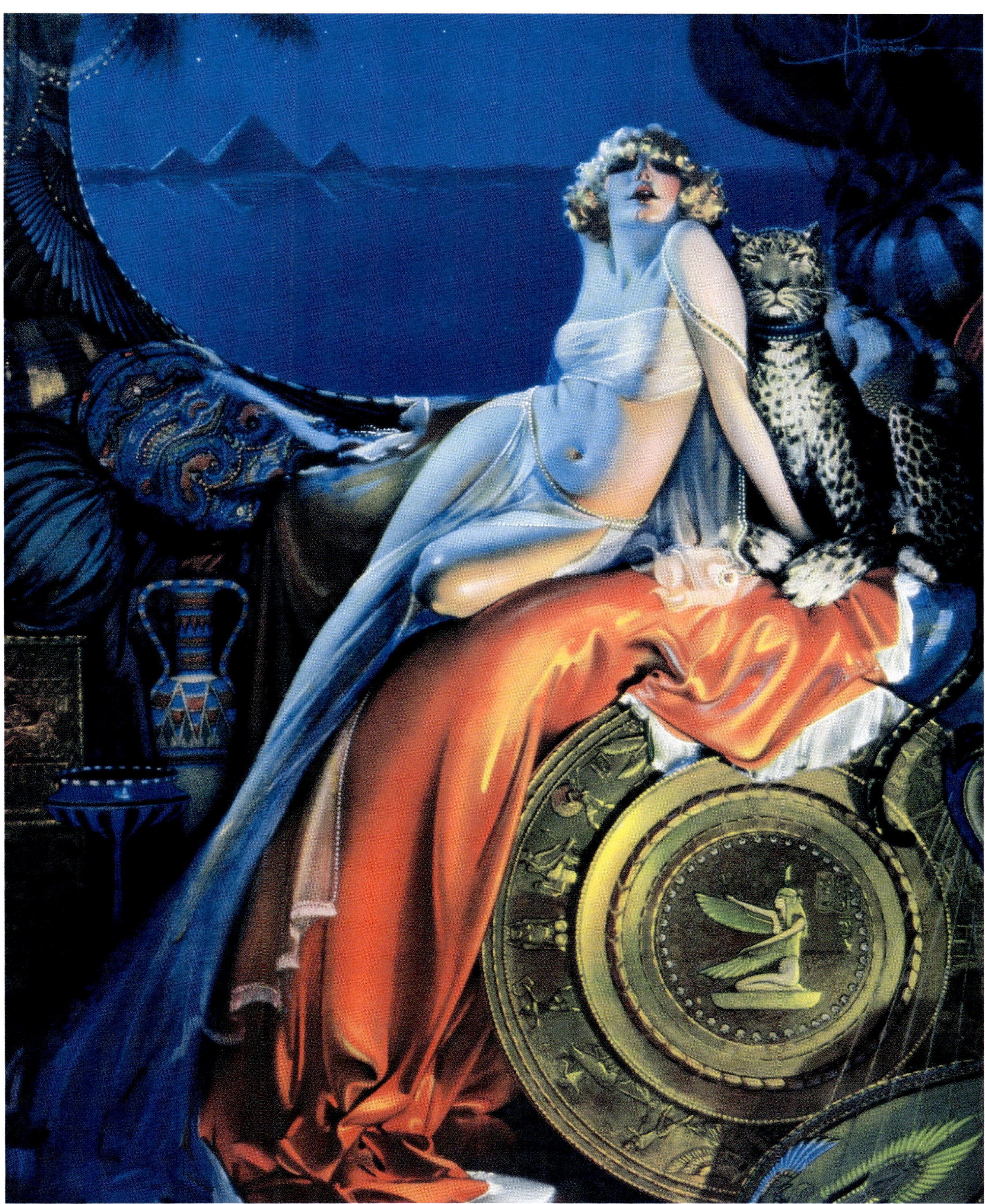

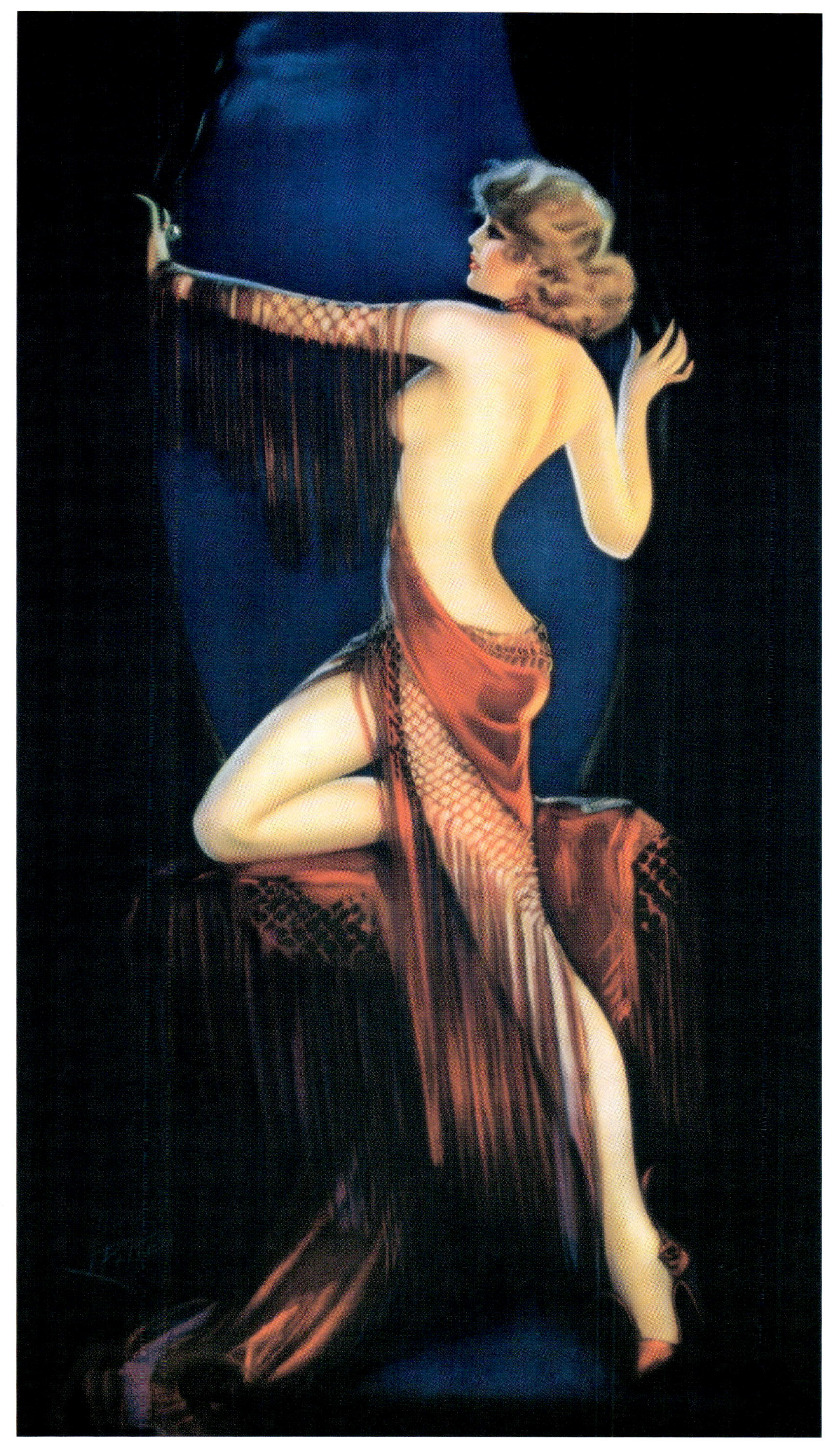

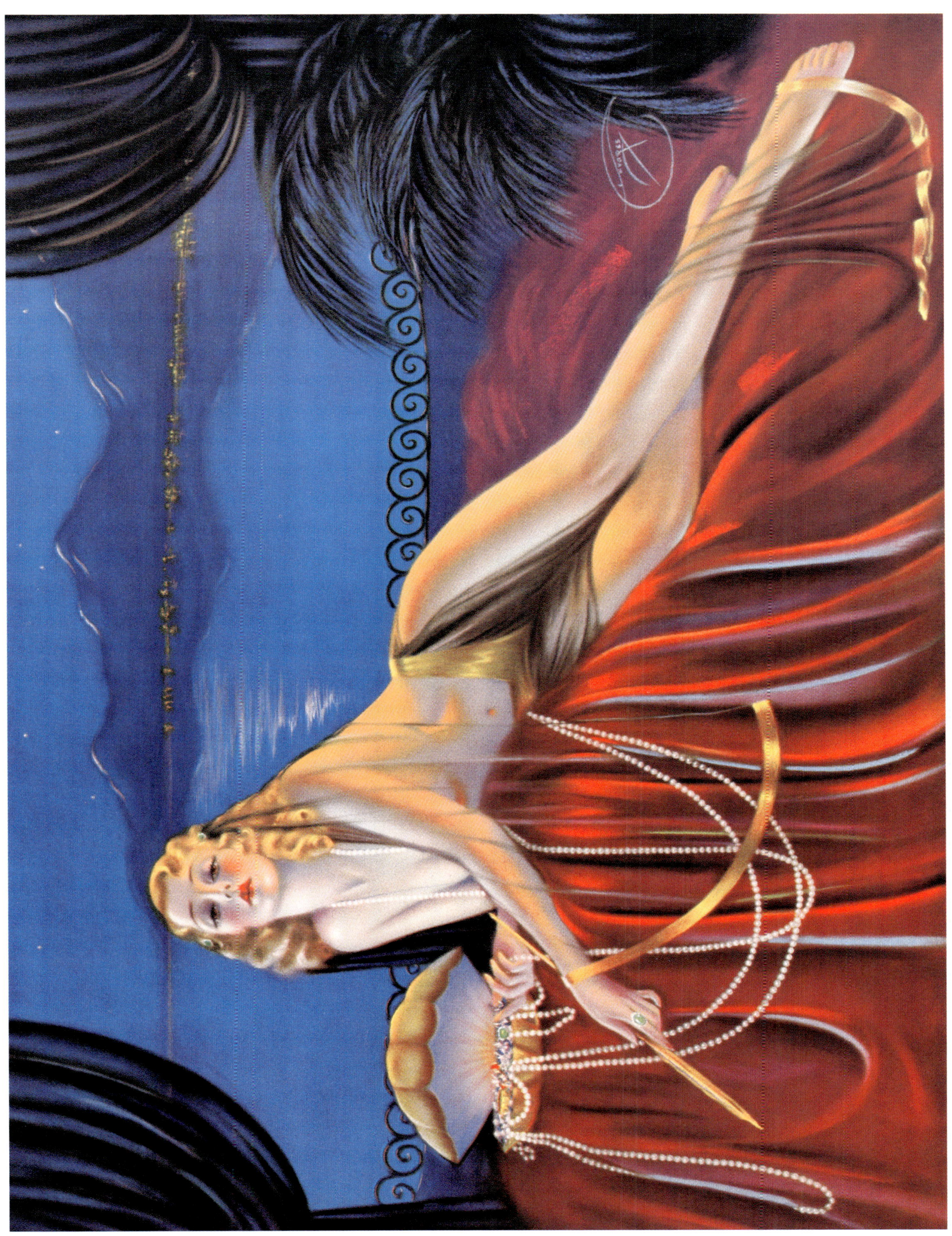

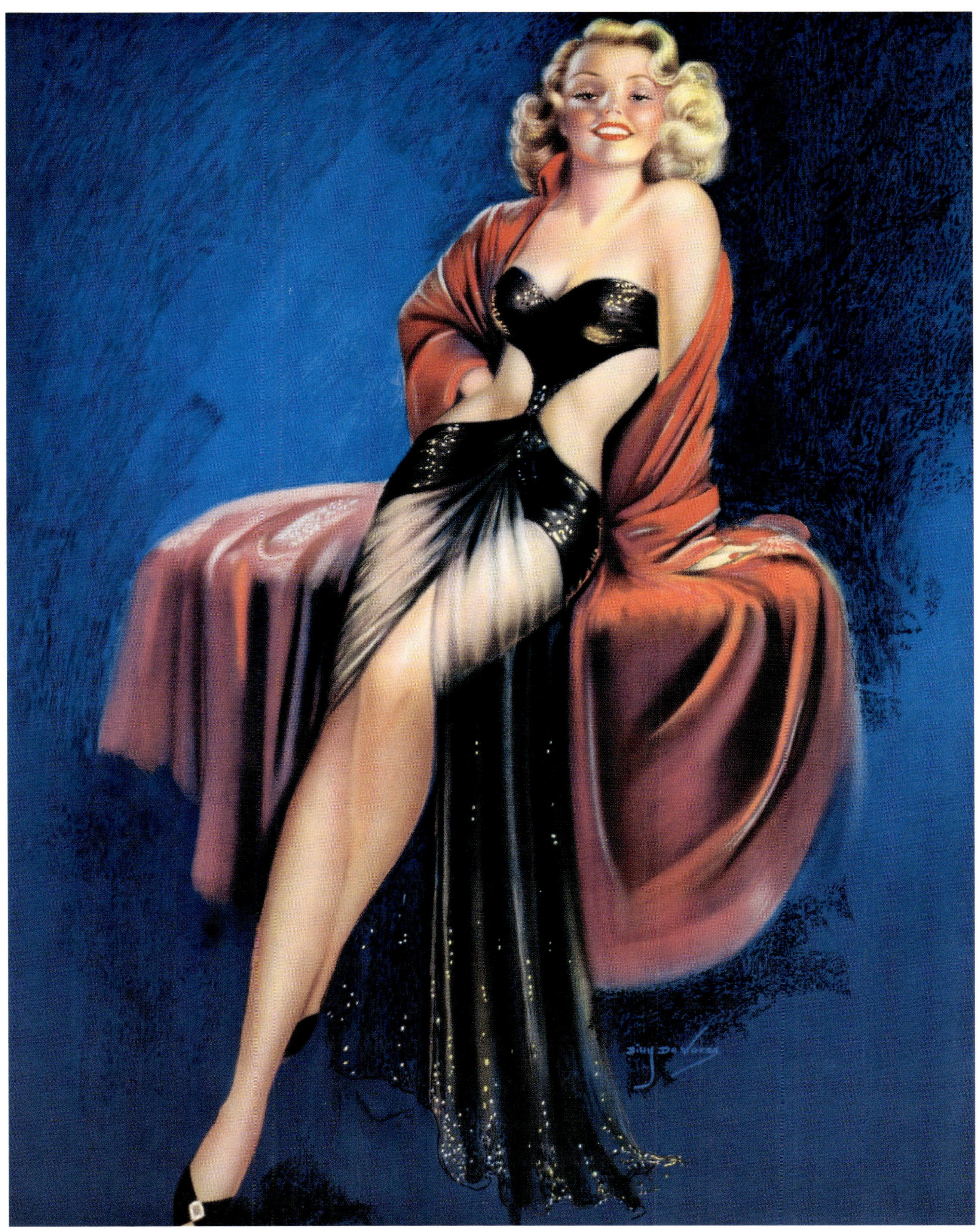

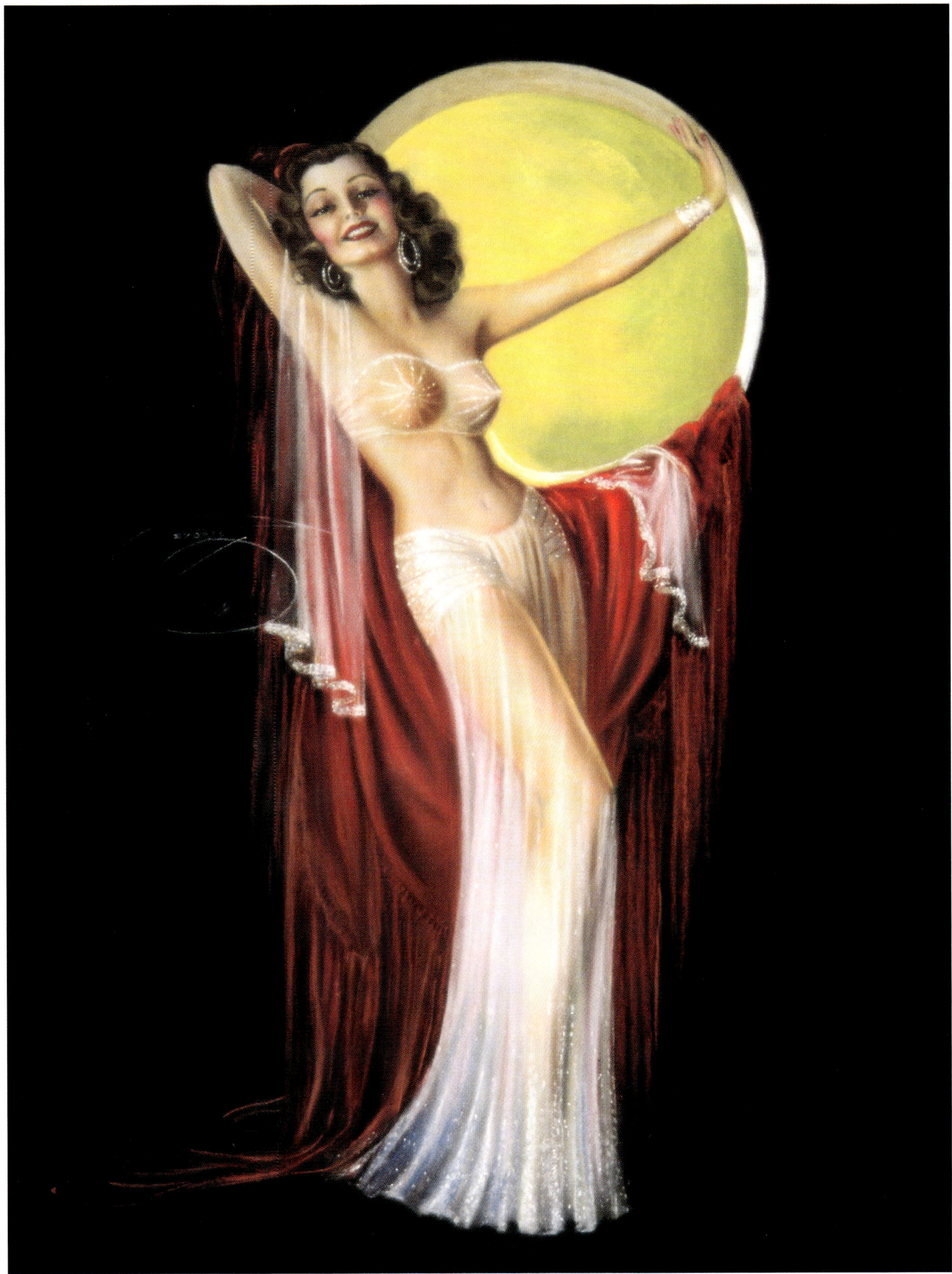

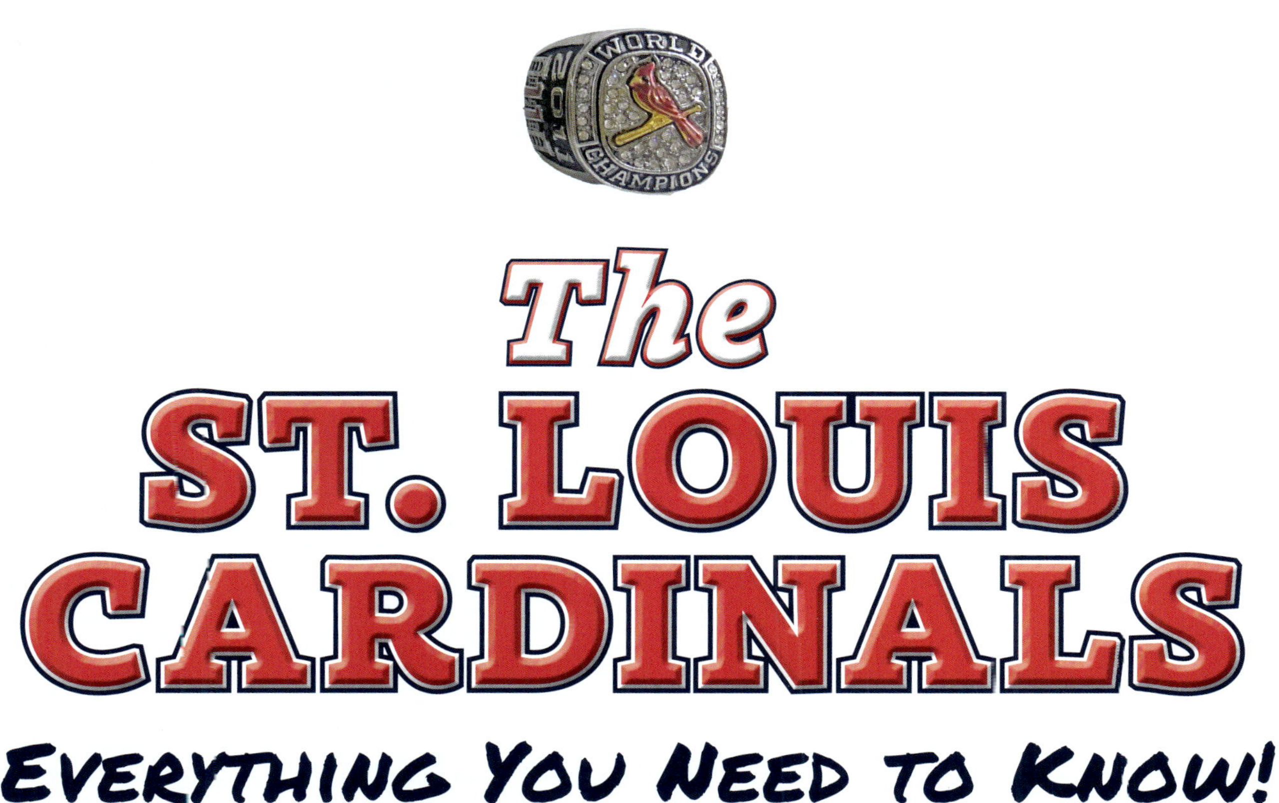

By Ed Wheatley

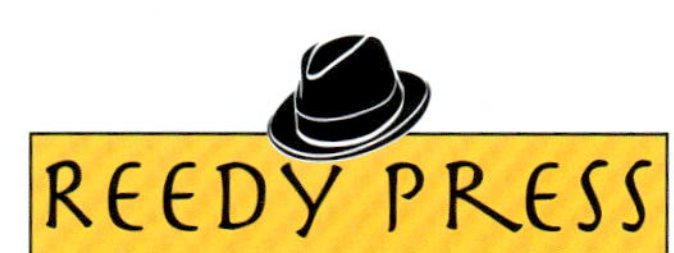

Reedy Press
PO Box 5131
St. Louis, MO 63139
www.reedypress.com

Cover Design: Eric Marquard
Interior Design: Eric Marquard and Linda Eckels

All cover photos courtesy of Getty Images.

All interior photos and memorabilia are courtesy of the author unless otherwise noted.

ISBN: 9781681064451

Library of Congress: 2023935093

Printed in the United States
23 24 25 26 27   5 4 3 2 1

Table of Contents

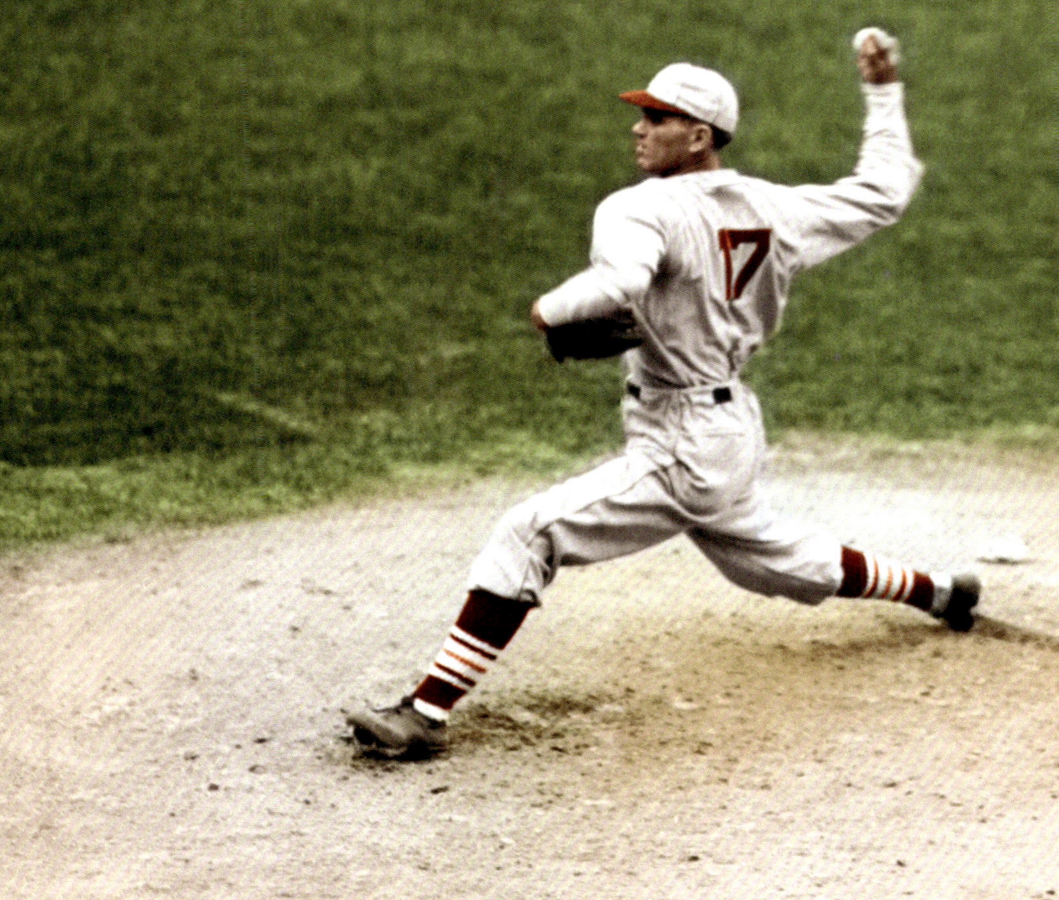

Dizzy Dean pitching for the St. Louis Cardinals against the Detroit Tigers in the 1934 World Series
Credit Getty Images

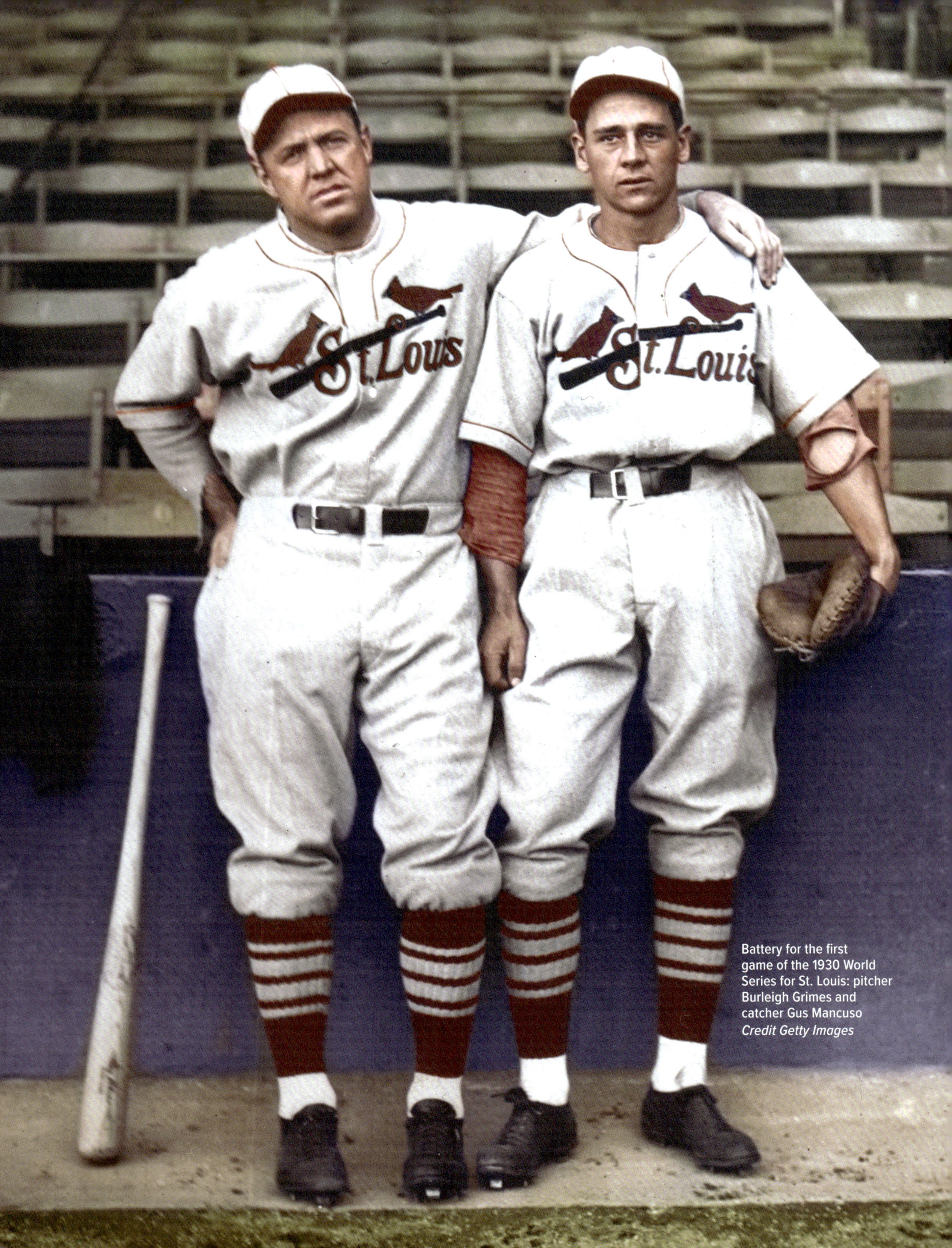

Battery for the first game of the 1930 World Series for St. Louis: pitcher Burleigh Grimes and catcher Gus Mancuso
Credit Getty Images

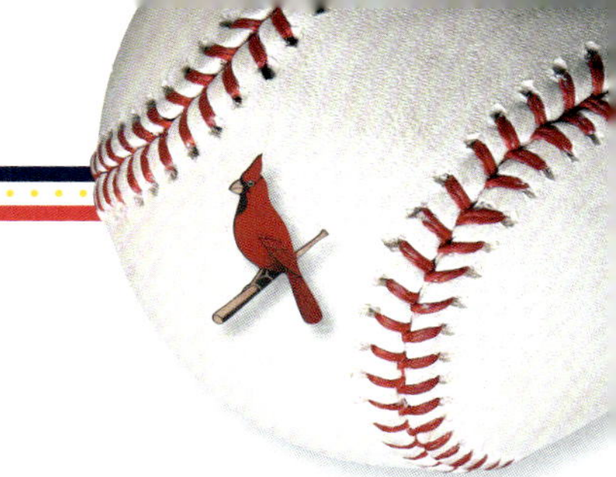

Introduction

St. Louis is regularly recognized by players and the media as the best baseball town in America. Since 1860, St. Louis summers have revolved around the beloved game of baseball. For over 140 of those years, the fans' focus has been on the baseball team that today we call the Cardinals.

St. Louis fans love Redbird baseball. Some say it's the city's true religion and "opening day" is the city-wide holiday. Cardinal fans are some of the smartest in the game. They are not just homers rooting only for their team and players. Should an opposing team's player make a great play, Cardinals fans will stand up, applaud, and cheer!

St. Louisans appreciate good baseball, and they've seen a lot of it. In all of baseball, only the mighty New York Yankees have won more world championships than the Cardinals. For many, the Cardinals have always been the antithesis of the New Yorkers. The Redbirds have played an exciting, rough-and-tumble style of baseball that resonates with their fans. Revisit that history, the teams, the players, and the moments told within these stories, pictures, and records that highlight the success of the "Cardinal Way." Root once more for the Cardinal heroes from the past and present while waiting for the next crack of the bat or the umpire's call of "play ball!"

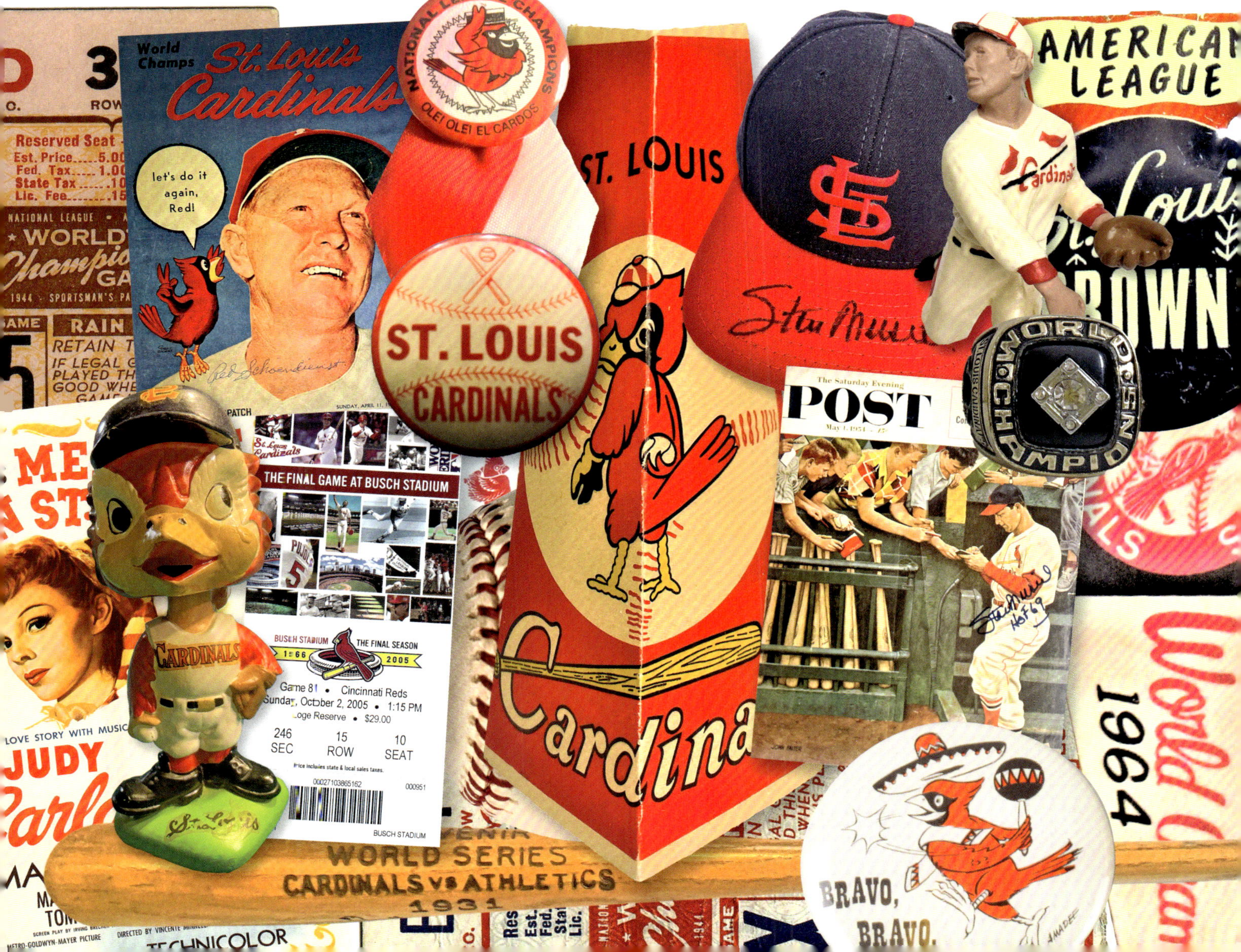

The Evolution of the Cardinals

They weren't always the Cardinals, and they weren't the first or the only team to ever play major league baseball in St. Louis. When they joined the National League (N.L.) in 1892, they weren't even called the Cardinals. They were called the Browns—a name that had been used by many teams prior to their 1892 entry and would be used by another St. Louis major league team during the 1900s.

The Birth of Baseball in St. Louis! Baseball as we know it today first came to St. Louis in July 1860—nearly a year before the Civil War and Abraham Lincoln becoming President. Baseball originated in Hoboken, New Jersey, in 1846, not in Cooperstown, New York as the myth would have fans believe. It swept across the nation as an amateur game with teams forming in communities, churches, and factories. As the game became more competitive, players were signed and paid to stay with a team. This was the start of professional baseball. America's first professional baseball team was the Cincinnati Red Stockings in 1869. By 1875, St. Louis had two professional teams, the Brown Stockings and the Red Stockings, playing in a league called the National Association. The league folded after just one year, but the Brown Stockings would soon be back.

The National League Forms! In 1876, the Brown Stockings became a charter member of the newly formed N.L. (of today's Major League Baseball). They were the first of three different St. Louis teams to play in the N.L. and have no lineage to today's Cardinals. They only played two seasons before being expelled from the league due to gambling and game-fixing issues that plagued sports throughout this time.

Still the Brown Stockings! Despite the demise of the original Brown Stockings, baseball remained popular in St. Louis. Chris Von der Ahe, a German immigrant in the beer business, saw baseball's potential as an entertainment venture and, more importantly, as a source of beer sales on hot summer days. He purchased an independent team also named the Brown Stockings along with their field called Grand Avenue Grounds—located on Grand Avenue, between Dodier and Sullivan, just west of his tavern. In time, the field would be renamed Sportsman's Park and then Busch Stadium I.

Credit Library of Congress

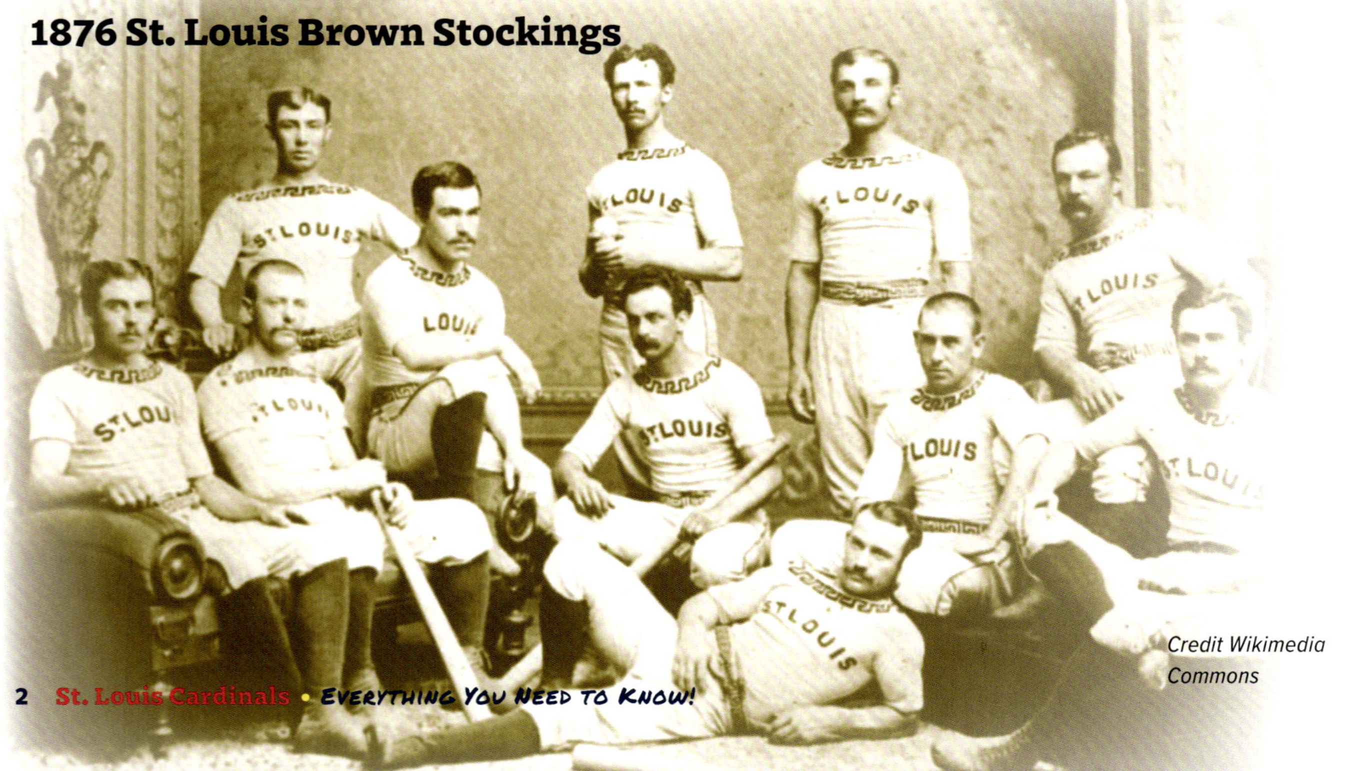

1876 St. Louis Brown Stockings

Credit Wikimedia Commons

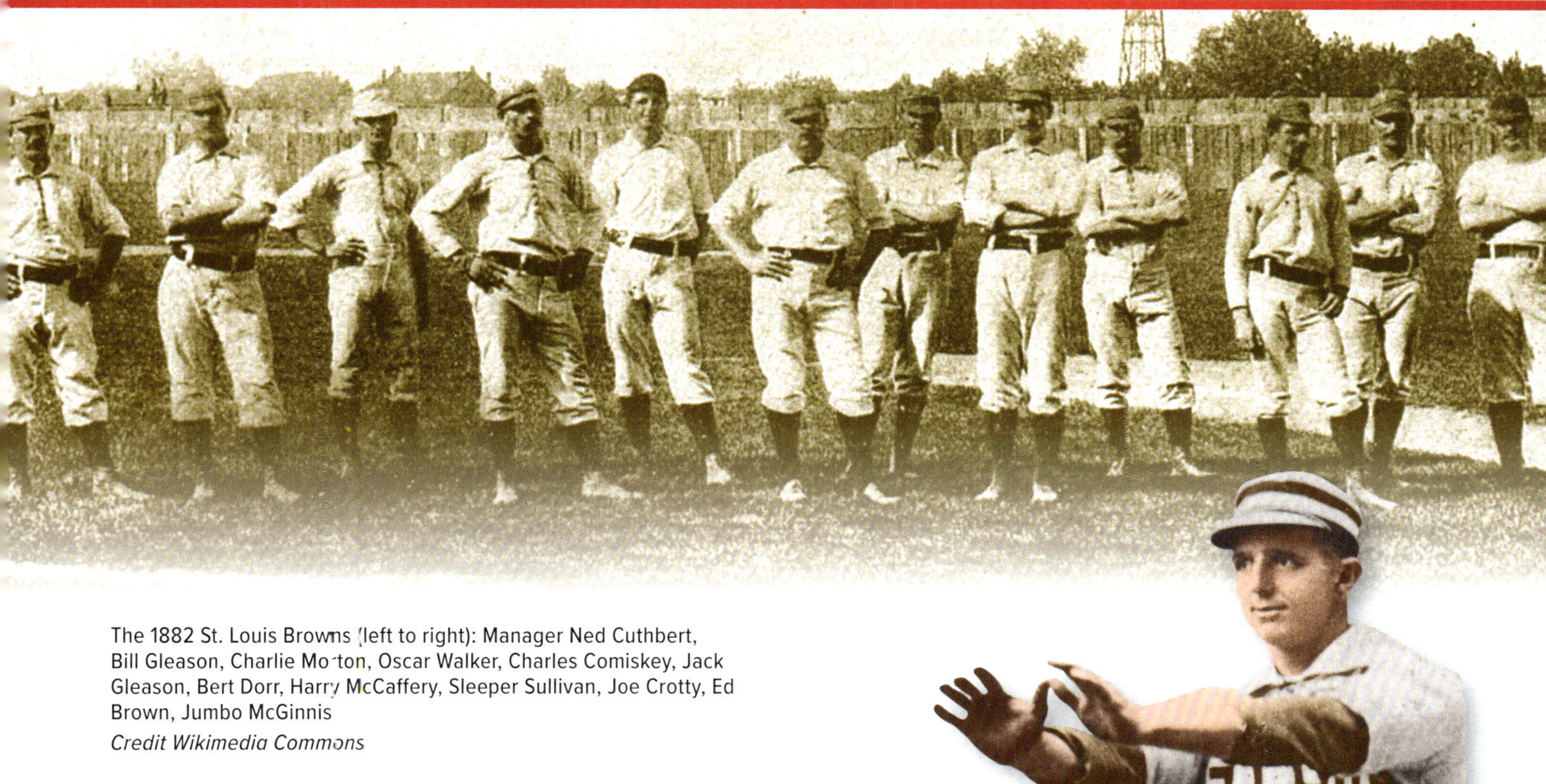

The 1882 St. Louis Browns (left to right): Manager Ned Cuthbert, Bill Gleason, Charlie Morton, Oscar Walker, Charles Comiskey, Jack Gleason, Bert Dorr, Harry McCaffery, Sleeper Sullivan, Joe Crotty, Ed Brown, Jumbo McGinnis
Credit Wikimedia Commons

Another League! In 1882, Von der Ahe's team joined a new league: the American Association (A.A.), formed to compete against baseball's N.L. Unlike the more puritanical N.L., the A.A. offered its fans a more rough-and-tumble game along with cheaper tickets, alcohol sales, and Sunday games.

Jealous of the Browns' success, the N.L. placed a rival team in St. Louis in 1885 called the Maroons to draw attention away from the Browns. The Maroons did not win over the city and ceased operations after the 1886 season. Would the N.L. ever come back to St. Louis?

The Third Time Is a Charm! St. Louis was the fourth-largest city in America, and the N.L. desperately wanted another team back there. In 1892, they invited Von der Ahe's successful Browns to move to the N.L. The Browns made the move and became the N.L. team fans still root for today!

A New Name Brings Success! In 1883, they became simply the "Browns" and were led by player-manager, Charles Comiskey. The Browns would rule the A.A. during the mid-1880s, winning four straight championships. In a precursor to today's World Series, the A.A. champion and the N.L. champion would meet in a world championship series. The Browns' 1886 win marked the only time an A.A. team would ever win this championship.

Charles Comiskey
Credit Wikimedia Commons

Pennants and Championships

With their 11 world championships and 19 pennants, the Cardinals have put together the best championship record in the National League. Only the New York Yankees with their 27 World Series titles and 40 pennants have won more championships in the history of the game. Interestingly, the Cardinals and Yankees have met five times in the Fall Classic and the Redbirds won three of those Series titles.

He Made Champions! The Cardinals would play 35 seasons before winning their first pennant in 1926. During those years, the team just wasn't very good (2,100 wins and 2,878 losses). That changed in 1919, when Branch Rickey joined the team and began developing good players with the creation of baseball's first farm system. Rickey's talent produced nine pennants over the next 21 years.

Credit Wikimedia Commons

It was the Cardinals' first World Series in 1926, but for their opponents, the New York Yankees, it was the fourth in the last six years. Nicknamed "Murderers' Row," the Yankees were a formidable opponent with a star-studded lineup led by Lou Gehrig, Babe Ruth, and Tony Lazzeri.

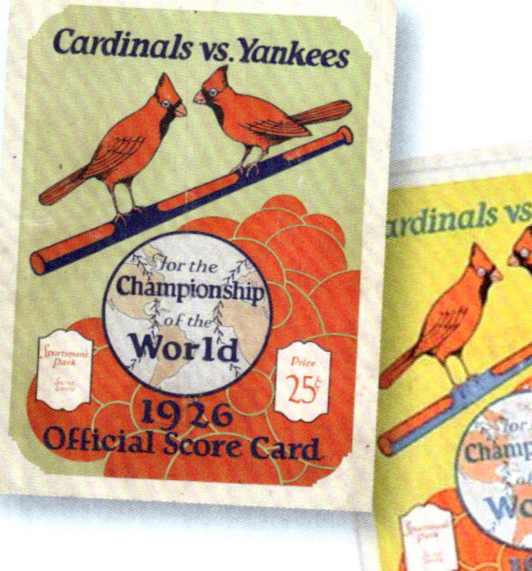

The two teams met again in the 1928 World Series. The Yankees had won the 1927 Series over the Pirates in a four-game sweep that capped Babe Ruth's record setting season of 60 home runs. They then defeated the Cardinals in 1928 in four straight games to sweep a second straight Series. Babe Ruth batted .625 in the Series and also hit three home runs in Game 4. Lou Gehrig batted .545 and hit four home runs in the Series.

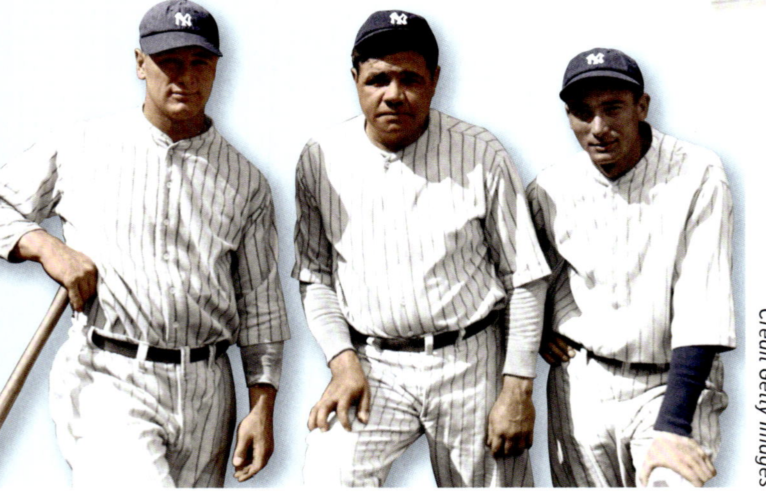

Credit Getty Images

Thanks to Rickey's player development, the 1926 Cardinals fielded a formidable team under their player-manager Rogers Hornsby. In a Series that seemed like "David versus Goliath," St. Louis shocked the baseball world by beating the Yankees in seven games for their first world championship.

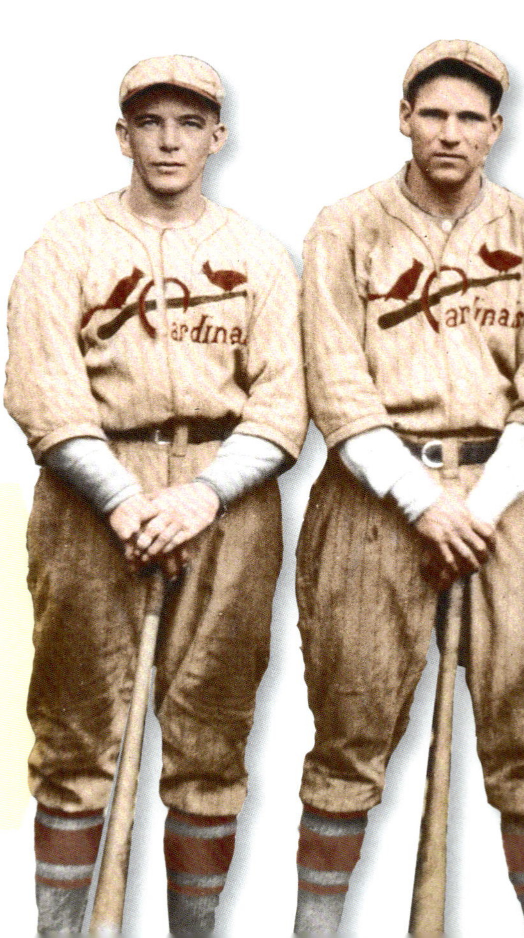

The 1926 St. Louis Cardinals, (left to right) outfielder Taylor Douthit, infielder Lester Bell, infielder Jim Bottomley, outfielder Chick Hafey, and catcher Bob O'Farrell.
Credit Getty Images

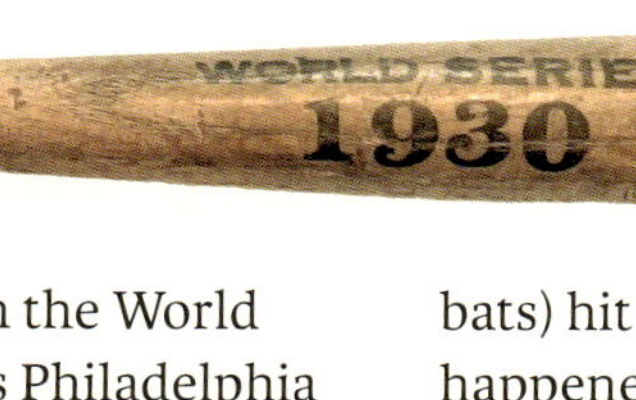

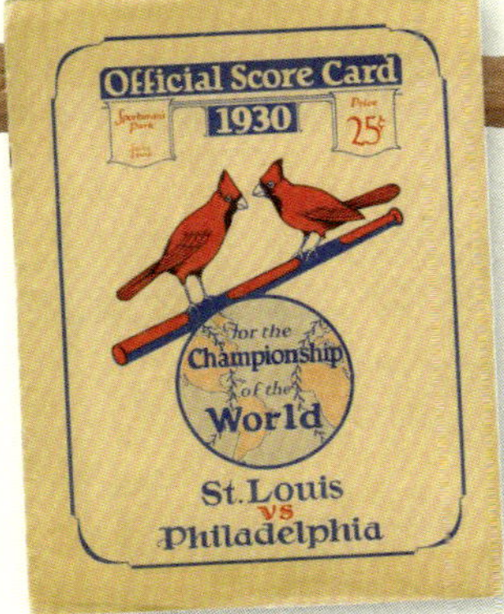

The Cardinals were back in the World Series in 1930. Connie Mack's Philadelphia Athletics dethroned the Yankees in 1929 and were looking to repeat as world champions. The Redbirds won the pennant with their hitting. Every hitter on the Cardinals that season (with over 300 at-bats) hit over .300—the only time that has happened in the history of the game. They also led the N.L. in scoring (six runs per game). However, in the Series, they only managed two runs per game, which helped the A's win the Series four games to two.

In a repeat of the previous year's Series, Connie Mack's "Mack Attack" sought a third straight Series title in 1931. It was not to be. The Cardinals won it all in seven games behind the hitting of Pepper Martin and the pitching of "Wild Bill" Hallahan and Burleigh Grimes.

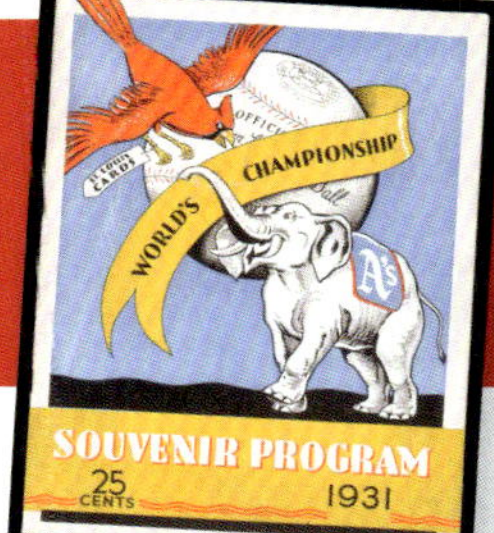

The Cardinals regrouped and won the pennant and World Series in 1934 with a rough-and-tumble group of players known as the "Gashouse Gang." Led by future Hall of Famers Frankie Frisch, Joe Medwick, and Dizzy Dean; the Cardinals won the World Series in seven games over the Detroit Tigers.

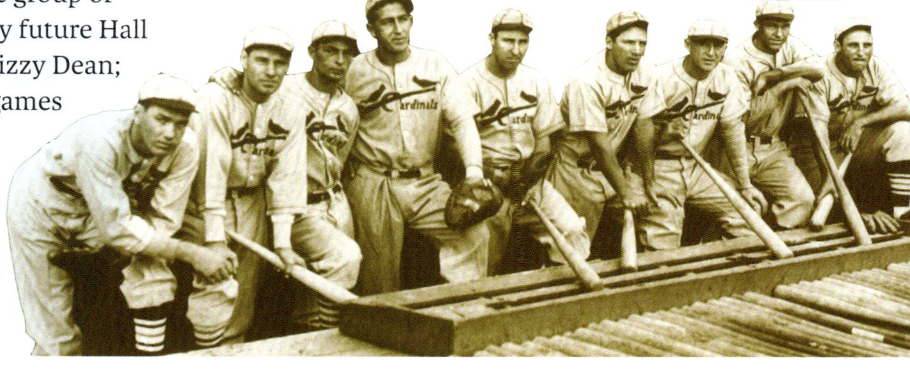

1934 Cardinals, (left to right) pitcher "Dizzy" Dean, shortstop Leo Durocher, center fielder Frank Orsatti, catcher Bill Delancey, first baseman Rip Collins, left fielder Joe Medwick, manager and second baseman Frank Frisch, right fielder Jack Rothrock, and third baseman Pepper Martin

Credit Getty Images

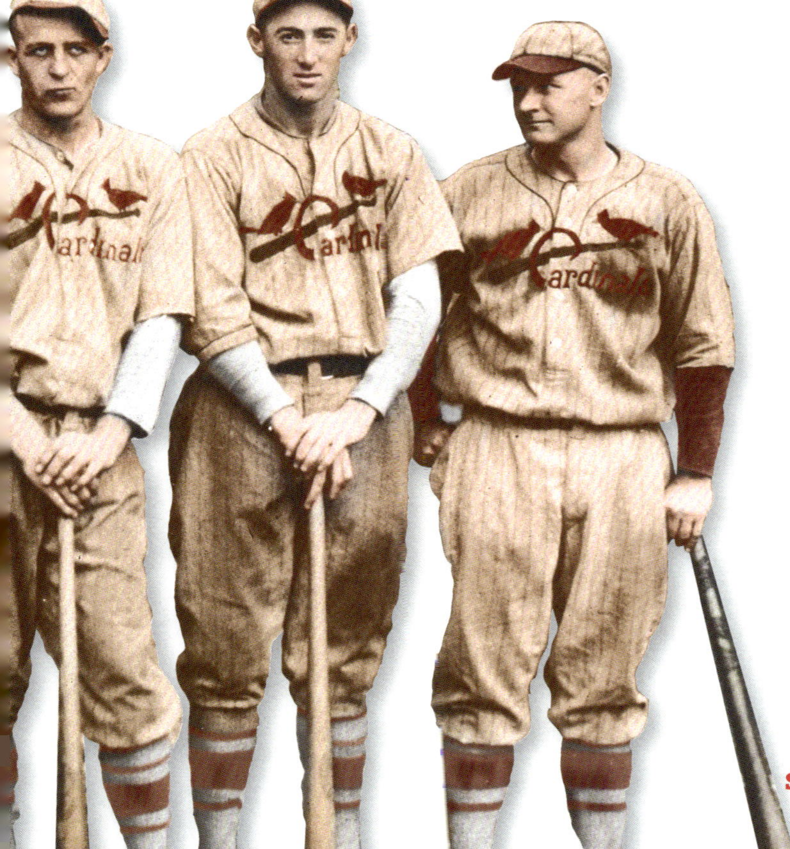

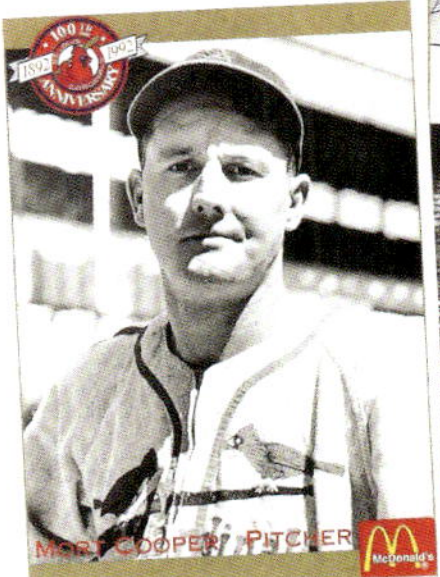

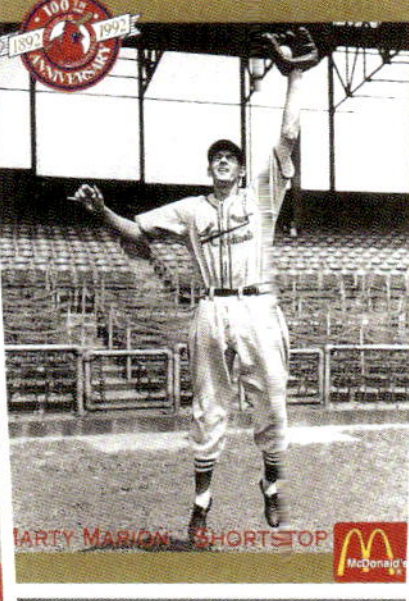

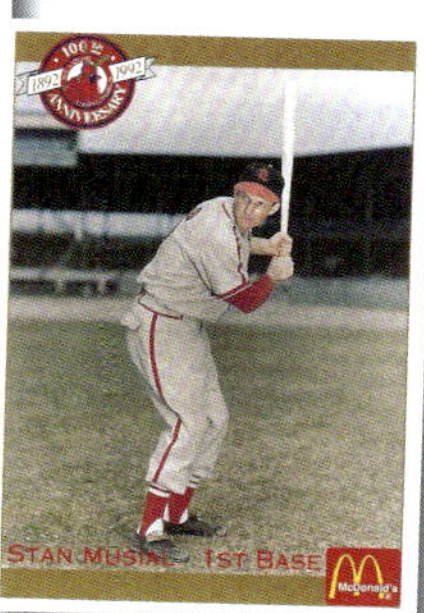

Four More! While they wouldn't win a pennant during the next seven seasons, the Cardinals did come in second four times. Then, from 1942 to 1946 they won four pennants and three World Series titles. Pitcher Mort Cooper won the 1942 N.L. MVP, and an up-and-coming star named Stan Musial won it the following year. In 1944, Marty Marion, the slick-fielding shortstop, was the MVP. That's three MVPs on three teams in three years, that won 106, 105, and 105 games respectively—quite a statement for Mr. Rickey's player development.

Pennants and Championships

In 1942, the Cardinals met the Yankees for the third time in the Fall Classic. The New Yorkers had won eight Series since the Redbirds had beaten them in 1926. After losing the first game, the Cardinals won the next four for the championship—payback for the New Yorkers' sweep of the Redbirds in 1928.

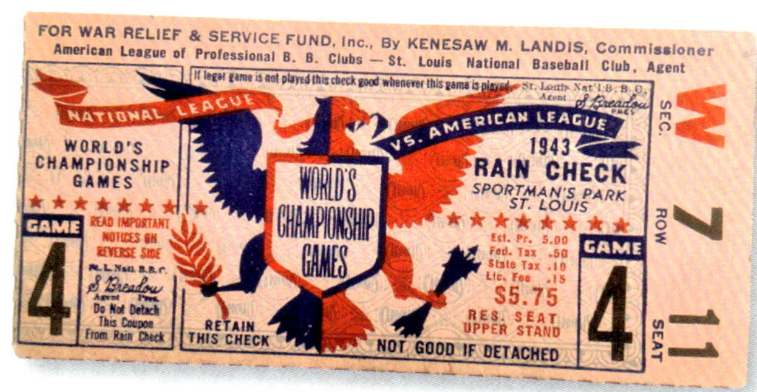

With many players off wearing military uniforms in 1943, the two teams met once more. Just like 1928, the Yankees won the encore, beating the Cardinals four games to one.

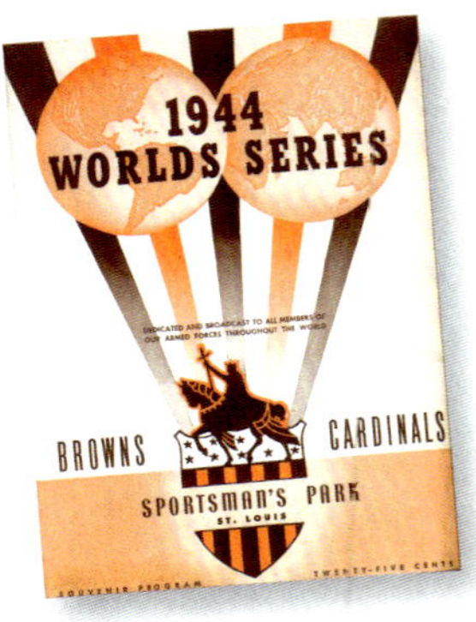

In 1944, the baseball world was singing the title song from the Judy Garland film, *Meet Me in St. Louis*, as the American and National Leagues' best teams were both from St. Louis. The St. Louis Browns had won their first and only pennant. The Cardinals had won their eighth and were stacked with three MVPs. It looked once more like a matchup between David and Goliath.

Credit Bill Howland Collection

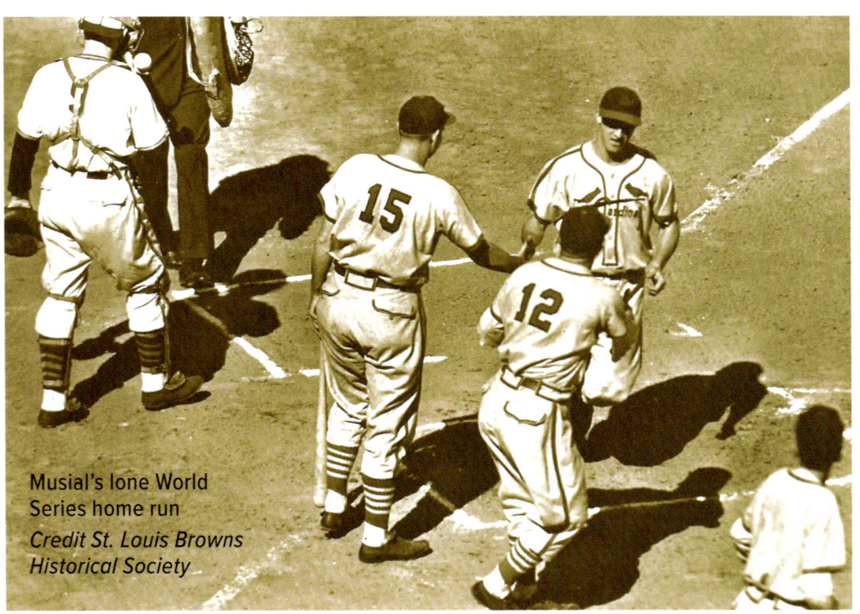

Musial's lone World Series home run
Credit St. Louis Browns Historical Society

The Browns got off to a quick start with a win in Game 1 and almost had Game 2 won until a key error by their pitcher allowed the Cardinals to come back and win in extra innings. The Browns won Game 3, but the Redbirds strength prevailed winning the next three games. Stan Musial would play in four Fall Classics, but he hit his only World Series home run in the first inning of 1944's Game 4.

A Tie! In 1945, Musial went off to war and the Cardinals finished in second place, two games behind the Cubs. In 1946, Stan was back and the Cardinals were back on top. The problem was they ended the season tied with the Brooklyn Dodgers and had to play baseball's first pennant playoff. The Redbirds won the best-of-three playoff series in two games and moved on to the World Series to play the Boston Red Sox.

Kurowski, Slaughter, Marion, and Musial
Credit Getty Images

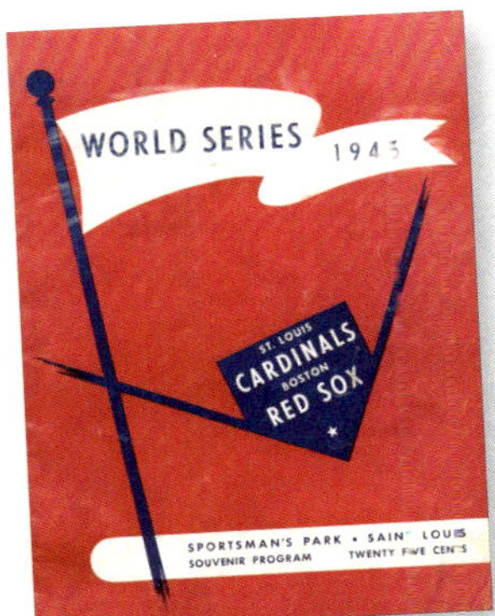

The 1946 World Series featured two of the game's best—the 1946 MVPs from both leagues—Ted Williams and Stan Musial. But neither of them was the Series' star. That would be a player named Enos "Country" Slaughter.

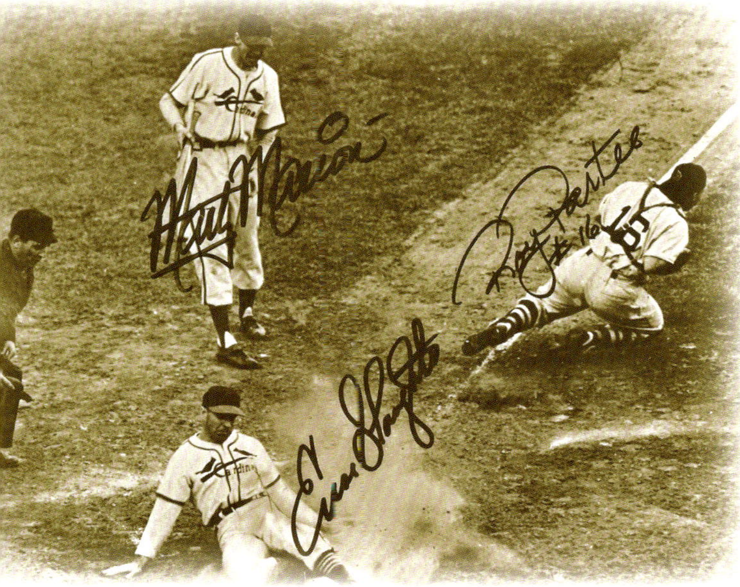

All the Way! Tied three games apiece, the championship would be decided in Game 7 at Sportsman's Park. It became one of the most epic Series finishes, known simply as "The Mad Dash." Tied 2–2 heading to the bottom of the 8th, Slaughter reached first base. With Slaughter running on the pitch, the next batter, Harry Walker, stroked a ball to center field and Slaughter never stopped running. He came all the way around, sliding into home plate to score the winning run of the game and the Series.

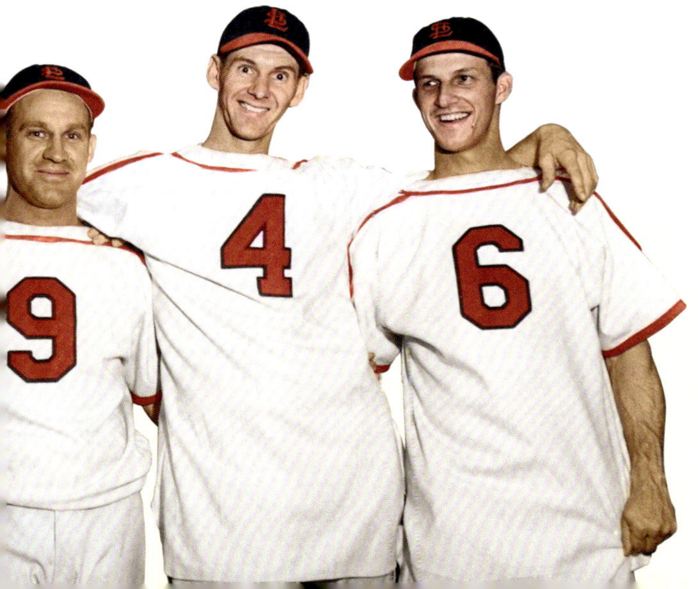

How They Stand

NATIONAL LEAGUE

	W.	L.	Pct.	G.B.
Philadelphia	76	47	.618	...
Cincinnati	69	55	.556	7½
San Francisco	69	55	.556	7½
CARDINALS	65	58	.528	11
Pittsburgh	64	60	.516	12½
Milwaukee	62	60	.508	13½
Los Angeles	60	62	.492	15½
Chicago	57	67	.460	19½
Houston	54	71	.432	23
New York	42	83	.336	35

AMERICAN LEAGUE

	W.	L.	Pct.	G.B.
Baltimore	77	48	.616	...
Chicago	76	50	.603	1½
New York	71	52	.577	5
Detroit	65	63	.508	13½
Minnesota	62	62	.500	14½
Los Angeles	63	66	.488	16
Cleveland	60	66	.476	17½
Boston	58	68	.460	19½
Washington	50	78	.391	28½
Kansas City	48	77	.384	29

August 1964 standings

How They Stand

NATIONAL LEAGUE

	W.	L.	Pct.	G.B.
Philadelphia	90	60	.600	...
CARDINALS	83	66	.557	6½
Cincinnati	83	66	.557	6½
San Francisco	83	67	.553	7
Milwaukee	77	72	.517	12½
Pittsburgh	76	72	.514	13
Los Angeles	75	75	.500	15
Chicago	67	82	.450	22½
Houston	62	89	.411	28½
New York	51	98	.342	38½

AMERICAN LEAGUE

	W.	L.	Pct.	G.B.
New York	89	59	.601	...
Baltimore	90	62	.589	1
Chicago	89	63	.586	2
Detroit	78	73	.517	12½
Cleveland	76	73	.510	13½
Los Angeles	77	76	.507	14½
Minnesota	75	76	.497	15½
Boston	68	84	.447	23
Washington	59	93	.388	32
Kansas City	54	96	.360	36

September 1964 standings

The Great Race! For most of the 1964 season, the Redbirds looked nothing like a pennant winner. On August 23rd, they were in fourth place trailing the Phillies by 11 games. Then the Cardinals started to win, and the Phillies started to lose. By September 20th, the Redbirds had tied the Reds for second place, but were still 6½ games behind the Phillies with just 12 games to play.

The ticket to the World Series came down to the last day of the season. That morning, it looked like there very well could be a three-way tie for the pennant between the Cardinals, Phillies, and Reds. The Cardinals and Reds were tied for first with the Phillies one game back. If the Phillies beat the Reds and the Mets beat the Cardinals, all would be tied. Fortunately, the Phillies beat the Reds and the Cardinals beat the Mets, so the Redbirds won the pennant.

Final Standings

NATIONAL LEAGUE

	W.	L.	Pct.	G.B.
CARDINALS	93	69	.574	...
Cincinnati	92	70	.568	1
Philadelphia	92	70	.568	1
San Francisco	90	72	.556	3
Milwaukee	88	74	.543	5
Los Angeles	80	82	.494	13
Pittsburgh	80	82	.494	13
Chicago	76	86	.469	17
Houston	66	96	.407	27
New York	53	109	.327	40

AMERICAN LEAGUE

	W.	L.	Pct.	G.B.
New York	99	63	.611	...
Chicago	98	64	.605	1
Baltimore	97	65	.599	2
Detroit	85	77	.525	14
Los Angeles	82	80	.506	17
Cleveland	79	83	.588	20
Minnesota	79	83	.488	20
Boston	72	90	.444	27
Washington	62	100	.383	37
Kansas City	57	105	.352	42

Final 1964 standings

Pennants and Championships

The Yankees and the Cardinals met in the 1964 World Series for the fifth time. The Redbirds had won in 1926 and 1942, while the Yankees had won in 1928 and 1943.

Lou Brock had come to the Cardinals from the Cubs mid-season 1964 and would energize the team's offense, while Bob Gibson became the team's pitching ace. From the first inning of the first game, the duo led the charge toward a seven-game 1964 World Series win and the Redbirds' seventh world championship.

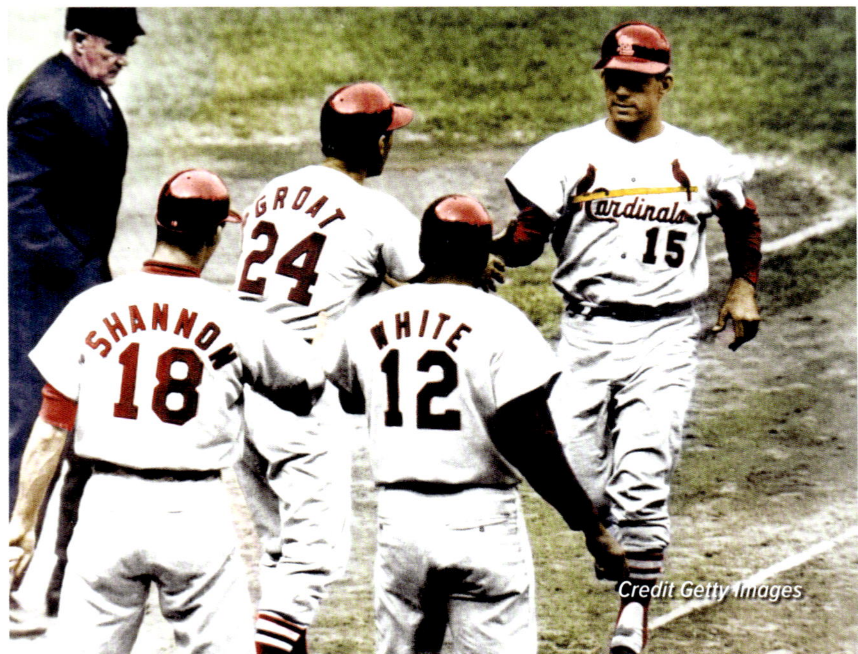

Credit Getty Images

The Cardinals were led by Ken Boyer, Lou Brock, Bob Gibson, and a cast of good players named McCarver, Flood, Groat, Shannon, and White.

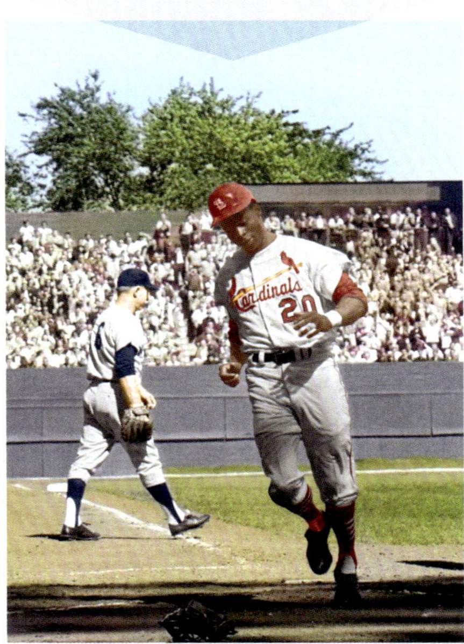

Credit Getty Images

Another Winning Trade! Just as the trade for Brock energized the Cardinals to the 1964 title, trades helped the Redbirds in 1967. Orlando Cepeda came from the Giants and would win the 1967 MVP. The Yankees' Roger Maris, a two-time MVP, was added to a lineup of Lou Brock, Curt Flood, Bob Gibson and an emerging Steve Carlton. Rallying around Cepeda's cries of "El Birdos" or "El Cardos," the Redbirds won 101 games and the pennant in 1967.

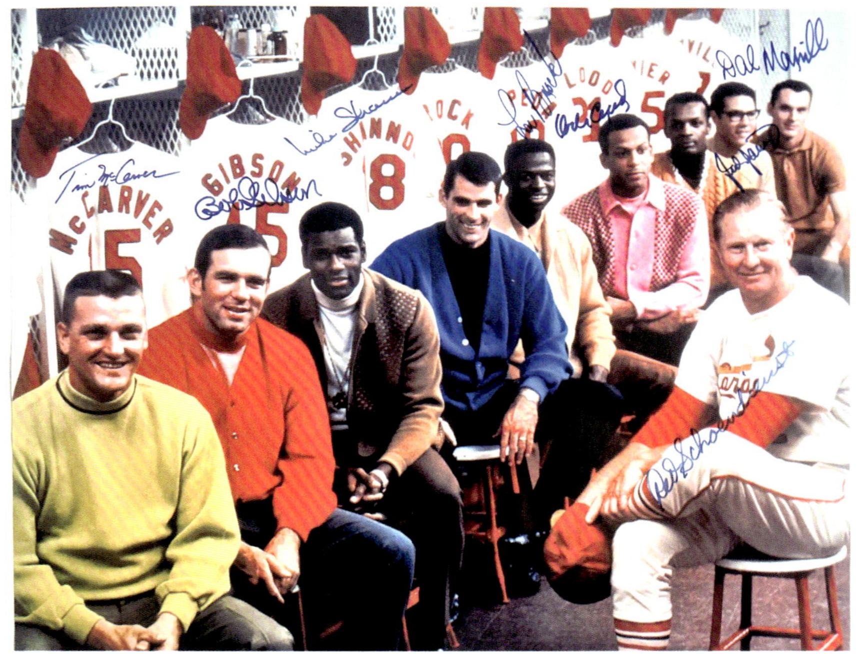

Credit Dr. Robert Wheatley

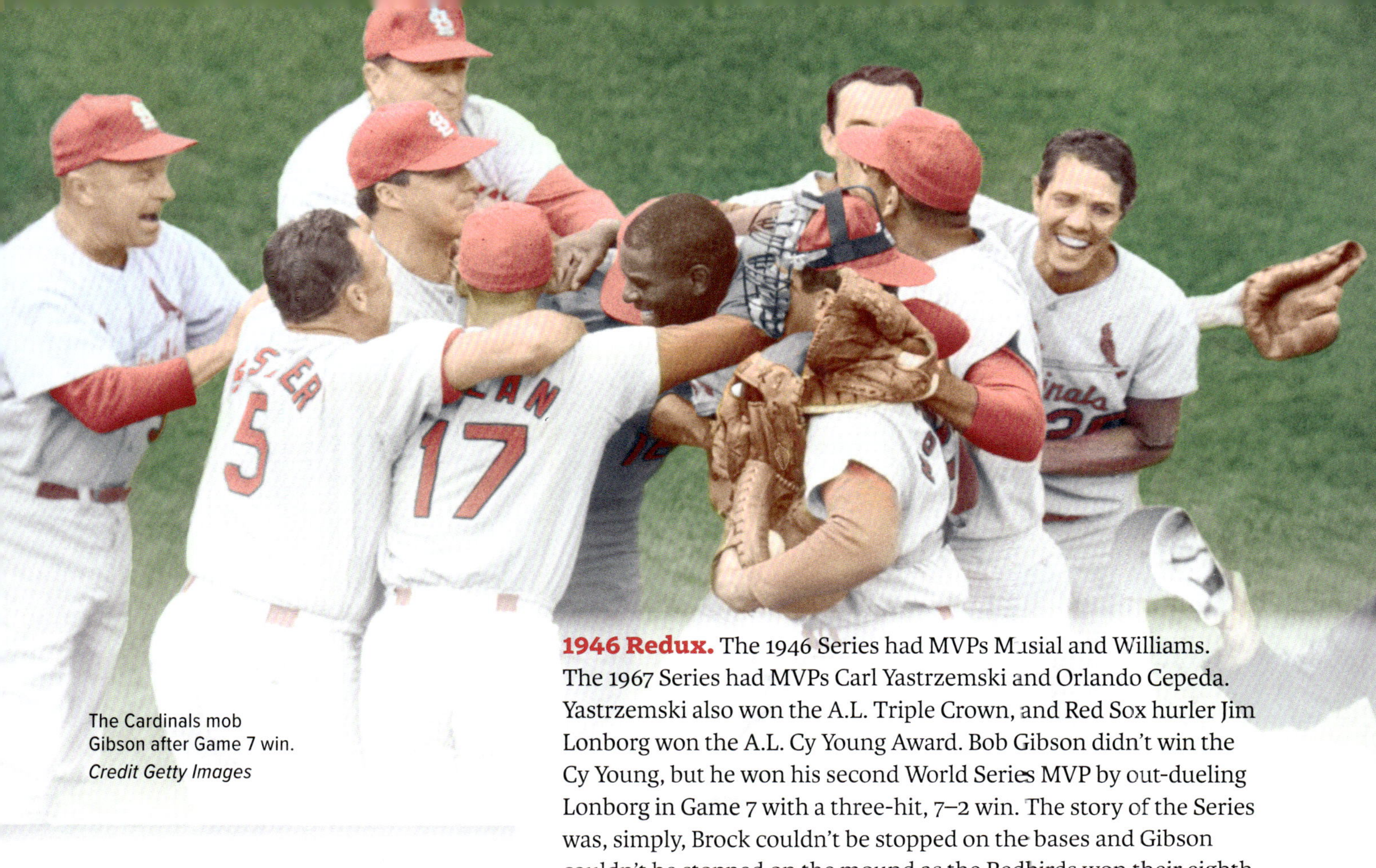

The Cardinals mob Gibson after Game 7 win.
Credit Getty Images

1946 Redux. The 1946 Series had MVPs Musial and Williams. The 1967 Series had MVPs Carl Yastrzemski and Orlando Cepeda. Yastrzemski also won the A.L. Triple Crown, and Red Sox hurler Jim Lonborg won the A.L. Cy Young Award. Bob Gibson didn't win the Cy Young, but he won his second World Series MVP by out-dueling Lonborg in Game 7 with a three-hit, 7–2 win. The story of the Series was, simply, Brock couldn't be stopped on the bases and Gibson couldn't be stopped on the mound as the Redbirds won their eighth championship title to go along with their 11th N.L. pennant.

The 1967 Series was a rematch of the 1946 championship with the Red Sox, still chasing the "Impossible Dream" of breaking the "curse of the Bambino"—a curse many believed prevented them from winning a World Series after Boston traded Babe Ruth to the Yankees following the 1919 season.

1934 Redux! 1968 was known as the "year of the pitcher." Bob Gibson would win the MVP and the Cy Young Award in the N.L. with a record-setting 1.12 ERA while the Tigers' 31-game winner Denny McLain also won both awards in the A.L. after becoming the first pitcher to win 30 games since Dizzy Dean in 1934.

Warren Giles presents Gibson with the Cy Young and MVP awards.
Credit Getty Images

The Redbirds easily repeated as 1968's N.L. pennant winners. They won the N.L. by nine games and found themselves facing their opponents from 1934—the Detroit Tigers.

A Gibby Redux! Gibson was dominant in the Series once more. In Game 1, he set a World Series record by striking out 17 Tigers in a 4–0 win. He got his seventh straight Series win in Game 4 to give the Redbirds a three-games-to-one Series lead. But the Tigers weren't destined to lose. They came back and won Games 5 and 6 to set up a Game 7 showdown—something Gibson had not lost in his previous two Series.

Pennants and Championships

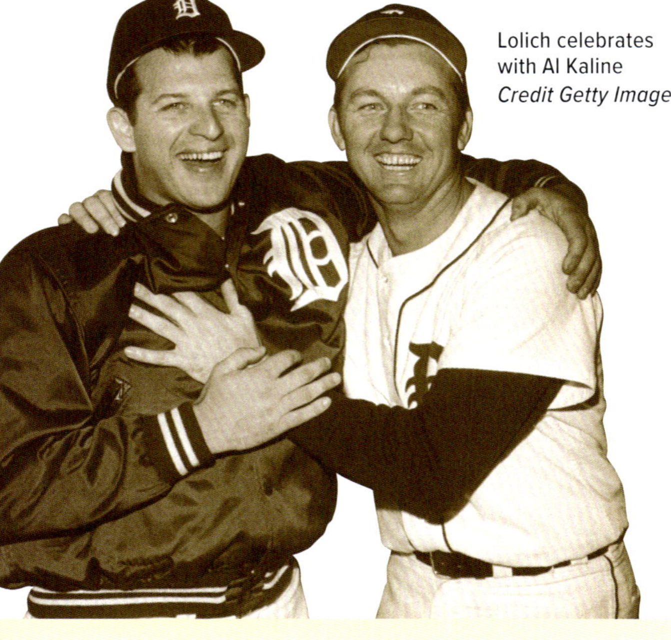

Lolich celebrates with Al Kaline
Credit Getty Images

Mickey Couldn't be Stopped! McLain was not the Tigers' ace in the '68 Series. Mickey Lolich was. He had beaten the Cardinals in Games 2 and 5 and would face Gibson in Game 7 for the win. Gibson did not give up a run until the seventh inning, when the Tigers got three runs on a misplayed ball by Curt Flood. Lolich only allowed a ninth-inning homer for a 4–1 win and a world championship.

Whitey Herzog became the team's manager and general manager in 1980. He built an exciting brand of baseball made for the Cardinals' spacious and astroturfed Busch Stadium II. Utilizing speed and defense, it became known as "Whiteyball."

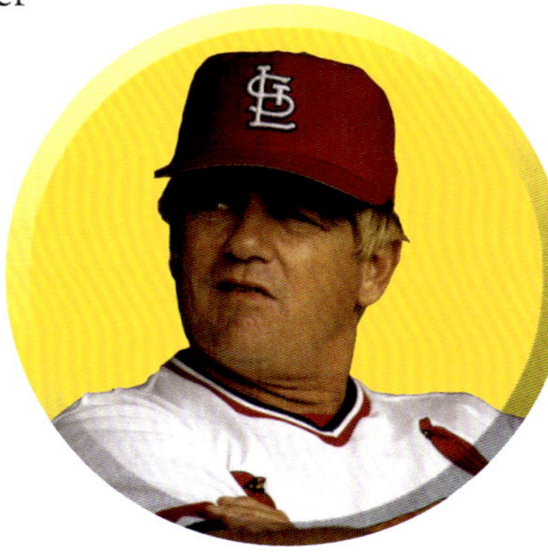

Credit Getty Images

Joaquin Andujar, Bob Forsch, and Steve Mura led the team as starters while Bruce Sutter closed out the games. George Hendrick, Tommy Herr, Keith Hernandez, Willie McGee, and the two Smiths—Lonnie and Ozzie—provided the offense. Darrell Porter led the team as the MVP in both the N.L. Championship and World Series.

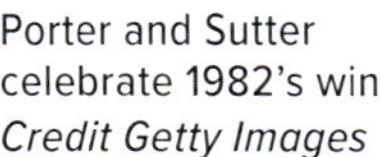

Porter and Sutter celebrate 1982's win
Credit Getty Images

"Celebration" became the theme song of 1982, as the team won their 13th pennant and ninth World Series. The Cardinals met the Milwaukee Brewers in 1982's Fall Classic (the Brewers would move to the National League in 1998). The two teams had made a preseason trade that positioned both to win their pennants and meet in the Series.

In 1985, the Cardinals won 101 games while their fans were dancing to the song, "The Heat is On." Willie McGee was the N.L. MVP, Vince Coleman stole 110 bases en route to winning Rookie of the Year honors, and new addition Jack Clark ripped 22 home runs. The team would outlast the Mets for the Division title and then the Dodgers in the playoffs before facing the Kansas City Royals in the "I–70 Series."

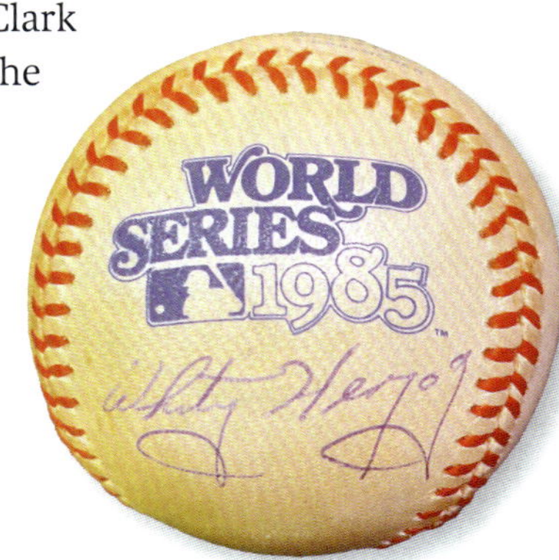

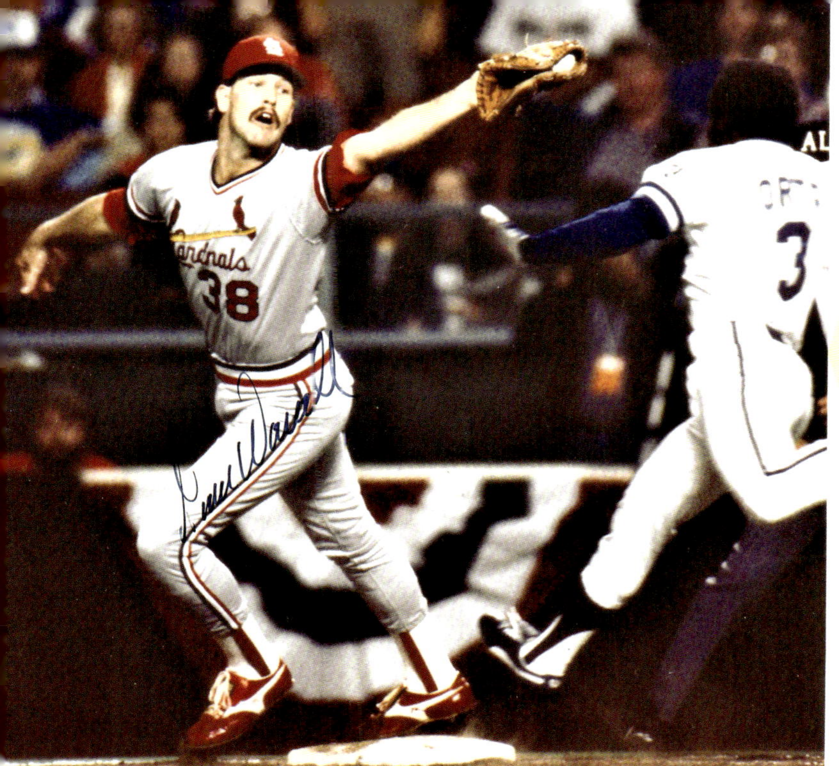

Upheaval! The '85 Series didn't end well. The mechanical tarp at Busch Stadium ran over Coleman's leg during the playoffs, leaving the team without their leadoff man's speed. Up three games to one, the Cards couldn't hold on. One singular play in Game 6 seemed to highlight the Redbirds' demise when umpire Don Denkinger missed a crucial call at first base that was then followed by a misplayed routine pop-up by Clark and Porter. As the ball fell, so did the Cardinals.

Tom Lawless
Infielder

In 1987 the Cardinals drew three million fans for the first time and won another pennant. 1986's Rookie of the Year, Todd Worrell, turned in another tremendous season out of the bullpen and Jack Clark lived up to his nickname, "the Ripper," with 35 homers. After besting the Giants in the playoffs, the Cards faced the Minnesota Twins in the first Series played indoors—a Series in which the home team won every one of the games. Too bad the Series didn't begin in St. Louis!

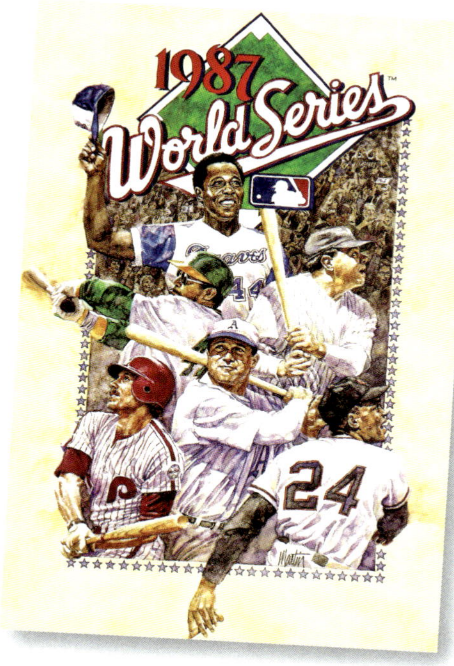

1987 was another Series in which the Cardinals were not at full strength. Clark and Pendleton were injured and offered little to the team's offense. Not even Tom Lawless's flip of the bat after a pinch-hit home run could flip the destiny of the Twins' first World Series championship.

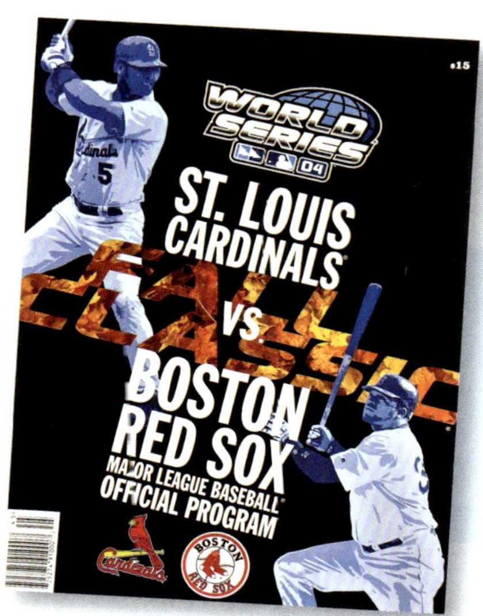

New ownership and a new manager in 1996 brought back the Cardinals' winning ways. Manager Tony LaRussa's team would lose four times in the playoffs before making it to the Fall Classic in 2004. The "curse of the Bambino" was finally lifted in the 100th edition of the World Series as the Boston Red Sox swept the Cardinals in four straight games. Not once during the Series did the Cardinals ever have the lead.

Pennants and Championships

Finishing 83–78 in 2006, the Redbirds made history as the team with the worst record to ever win a World Series. The Cardinals squeaked into the playoffs on the last day of the season thanks to a loss by the Houston Astros. They rallied past the San Diego Padres and New York Mets in the playoffs, and once more found themselves facing the Detroit Tigers in the Series.

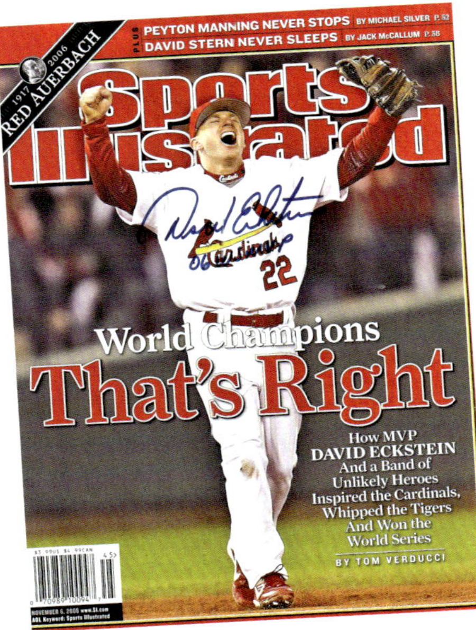

Payback for 68! Detroit had gotten to the Series based upon their strong pitching led by Justin Verlander and Kenny Rogers. But Redbirds rookie Anthony Reyes shut down the Tigers in Game 1 while Chris Carpenter, Adam Wainwright, and Jeff Weaver shouldered the other wins as the Redbirds won the series in just five games. The spark plug and hero of the Series was Redbird shortstop David Eckstein, who took home the World Series MVP.

One for the Ages! The 2011 edition of the Series became one of the most epic in history thanks to the bats of Cardinals third baseman David Freese and Albert Pujols. The teams split the first two games before Pujols blew open Game 3 with three home runs. Texas then won the next two games and was set to win the Series with a win in Game 6. That is, until David Freese came to bat!

The Cardinals made it back to the Fall Classic the hard way in 2011, as a "Wild Card." After losing Adam Wainwright for the season, they acquired Lance Berkman and Raphael Furcal to help the offense. The Redbirds got past the Phillies and Brewers before meeting the Texas Rangers in the World Series.

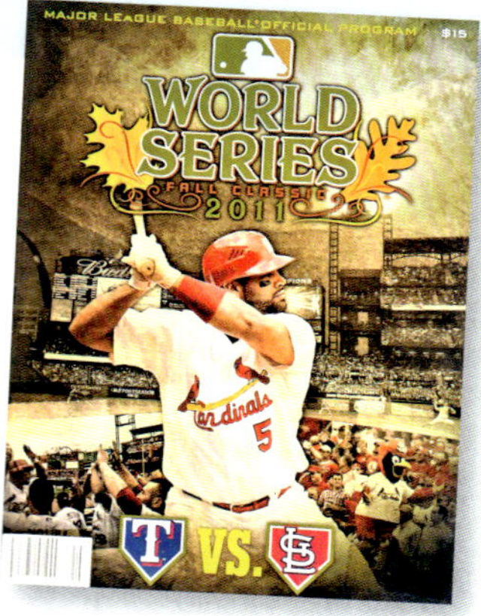

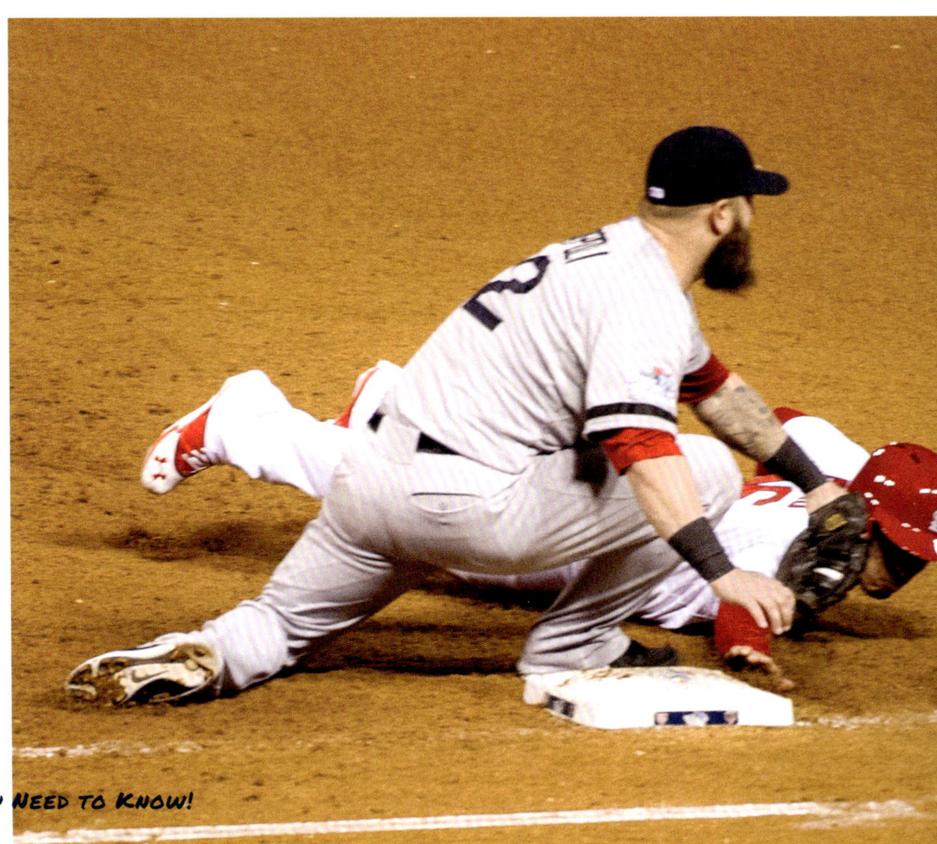

The Best Game Ever! That's the term used to describe Game 6, of the 2011 World Series between the Cardinals and Rangers. After the visiting Rangers scored first in the top of the first inning, the lead would change six times. With the Rangers up 7–5 in the bottom of the ninth and David Freese at bat with two outs, two strikes, and two runners on base, the Rangers were just a strike away from a world championship. But Freese didn't make an out. He tripled and tied the game 7–7. In the 10th inning, the Rangers got two runs and again were ready to celebrate a championship. But once more with two outs and two strikes, Lance Berkman singled home the tying run in the bottom of the inning. With the game still tied 9–9 in the 11th, David Freese sent a walk-off home run to centerfield to send the Series to Game 7.

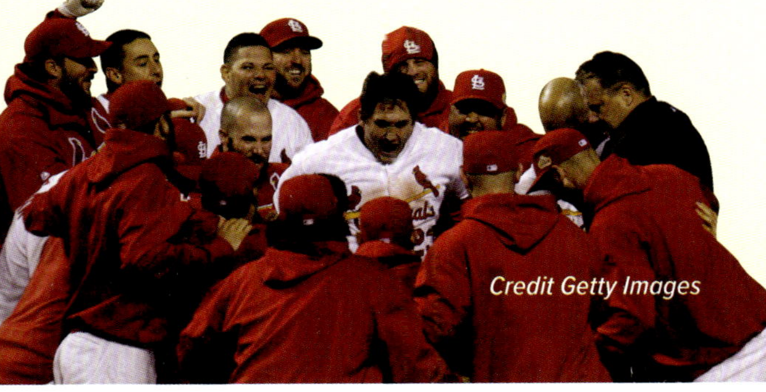
Credit Getty Images

Alan Craig
Credit Getty Images

Freese Frame! David Freese did it again in Game 7 with a game tying two-run double in the first inning. Alan Craig then put the Cardinals on top for good with a homer in the third and then ended a Texas rally by going high over the wall to take away a home run. The Cardinals held on for their 11th world championship.

The Cardinals were up two games to one entering 2013's Game 4, but the Red Sox took the next three games for the championship. The pivotal moment of the Series occurred in the 9th inning of Game 4. Boston closer Koji Uehara picked off Cardinals' pinch runner Kolten Wong to stop a Redbird rally, marking the first postseason game in baseball history to end on a pickoff. However, it was not the first time a World Series game ended with a runner being tagged out during an at-bat. In the 1926 World Series, Babe Ruth was caught stealing for the final out of Game 7. Although the Cardinals got to hoist their 19th pennant, they have yet to get their 12th World Series championship.

Credit Getty Images

After the 2011 celebration, Tony LaRussa retired and Albert Pujols left for the California Angels. The Cardinals added the offensive muscle of Carlos Beltran and Matt Holliday to the holdovers from 2011 for one more Series run under new manager Mike Matheny. In 2013, the Redbirds got past the Pirates and Dodgers in the playoffs to meet the Boston Red Sox in the Series for the fourth time.

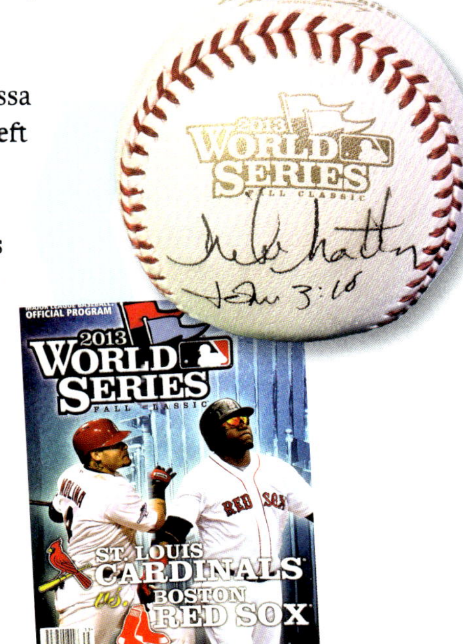

Memories and Moments

Across the storied franchise known today as Cardinal baseball, there have been many memorable moments since that first pitch was thrown in 1882. Many baseball fans create lists of baseball's greatest moments, players, or games. It is not surprising that many on these lists have ties to the Cardinals franchise.

Their rivalry goes back to 1885, before the two teams bore their current franchise monikers. The American Association Champion St. Louis Browns met the National League Champion Chicago White Stockings (original Cubs name) in what would be a precursor to today's World Series. That championship became engulfed in controversy and would end in a tie. The next time they met was on April 12, 1892, in St. Louis's first National League game, a 14–10 loss to the Chicago Colts (today's Cubs).

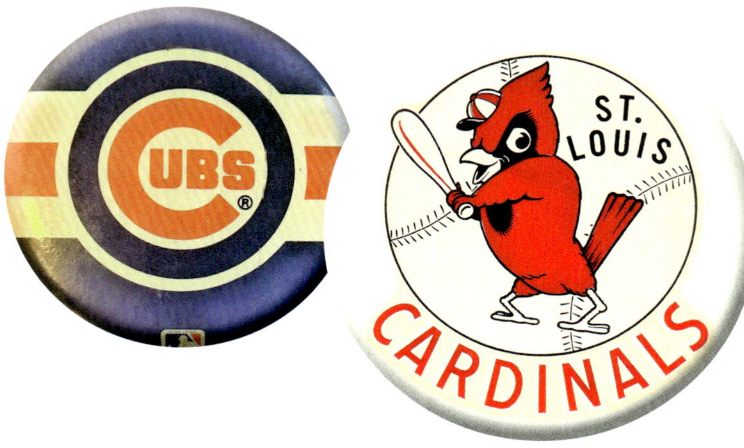

The Beginning of a Rivalry! There are many rivalries in baseball. Red Sox and Yankee fans like to think theirs is the best. Prior to 1958, the Dodgers and Giants battled as crosstown rivals in the boroughs of New York and still do so today in California. But has there ever been a longer and greater rivalry than that of the Chicago Cubs and the St. Louis Cardinals?

Alexander the Great! Although only pitching for four seasons for the Cardinals toward the end of his 20-year career, Grover Cleveland Alexander had one of those moments in the sun that stands out even in his Hall of Fame career. It happened in the 1926 World Series. Alexander had already pitched two complete game victories in Games 2 and 6. After the latter game, rumor has it that Alexander had "a night on the town" and came to Game 7 in no shape to pitch, or so it seemed. In the seventh inning, the Redbirds' razor thin 3–2 lead over the Yankees seemed doomed. Cards pitcher Pop Haines developed a blister and could no longer pitch. He left the game with two outs and the bases loaded. Coming to bat was hard-hitting Tony Lazzeri. Alexander was summoned to the mound to get an out and preserve the lead. Alexander's first pitch was a ball and then a strike. Lazzeri then crushed a ball toward the left field pole—just foul. Alexander had him set up and then got him with a swing and a miss to crush the rally. Alexander then blanked the New Yorkers in the eighth and ninth innings, and the Cardinals got their first world championship.

Credit Getty Images

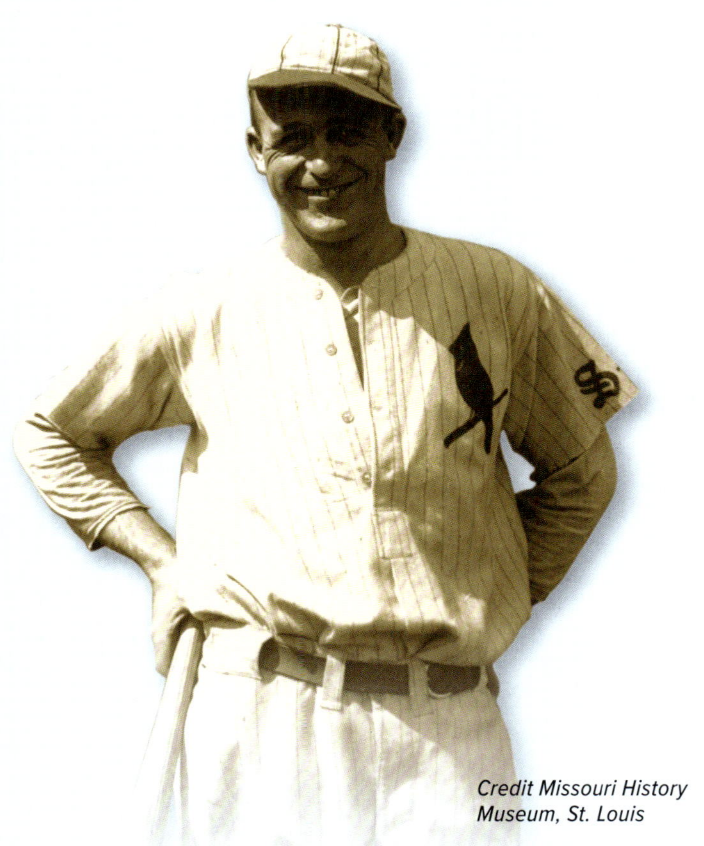

Credit Missouri History Museum, St. Louis

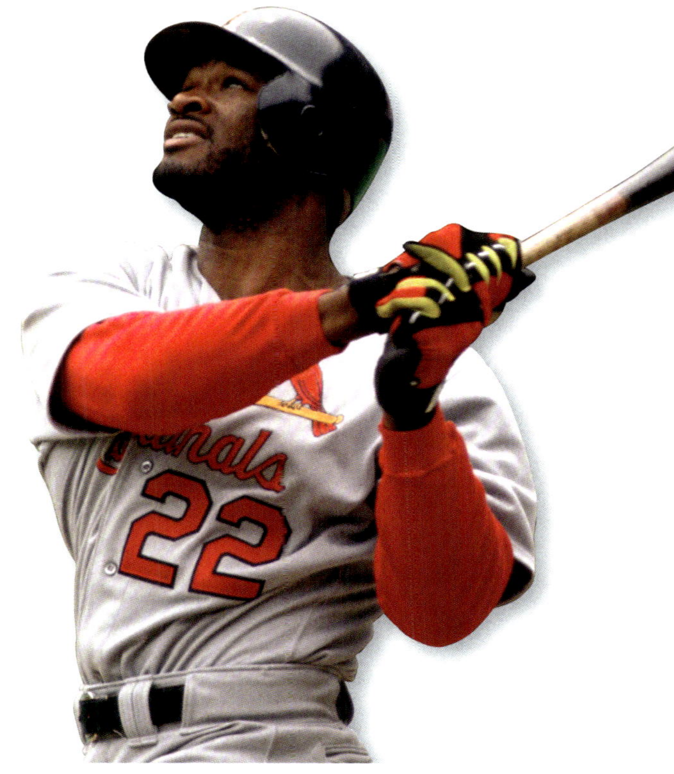

Jim and Mark's Record Days! "Sunny Jim" Bottomley was the Cardinals cleanup hitter anchoring the great teams of the 1920s. For five seasons between 1925 and 1929 Bottomley had more than 120 RBI, twice leading the league. Playing against the Brooklyn Robins (Dodgers) on September 16, 1924, he set a major league record of 12 RBI in a single game. He accomplished the feat by hitting two home runs, a double and three singles as he went 6-for-6 at the plate.

Bottomley's record would stand untouched for 69 years until 1993, when "hard hittin'" Mark Whitten also drove in 12 runs for the Cardinals. Whitten accomplished the feat with just four swings against the Cincinnati Reds on September 7, 1993. He hit a grand slam in the first inning, three-run homers in the sixth and seventh innings, and then a two-run homer in the ninth.

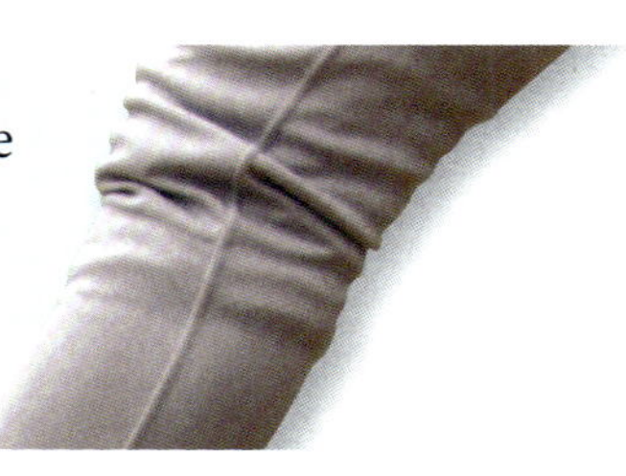

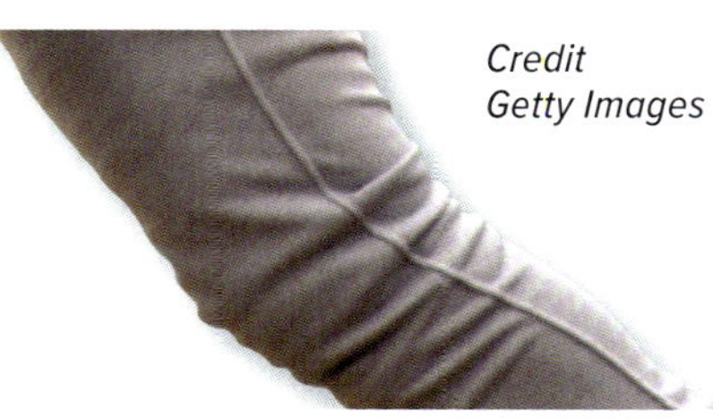

Credit Getty Images

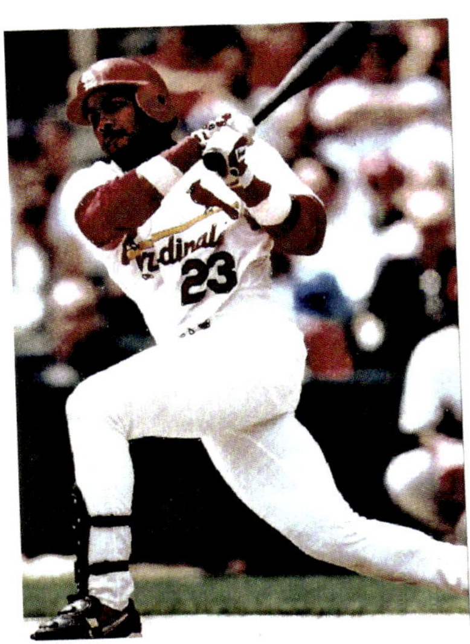

Fernando Tatis Makes Baseball History

Fernando Tatis belted two grand slam home runs in the same inning, a first in Major League Baseball history. Both shots came off Chan Ho Park in the 3rd inning, as Tatis's 8 RBI surpassed the MLB one-inning record by two. Park became the first pitcher this century and only the second ever to allow two grand slams in an inning. The Cardinals won 12-5.

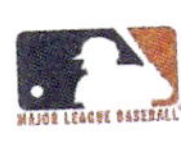

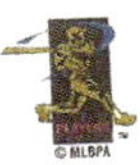

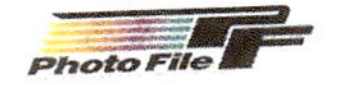

Two in One! It wasn't 12 RBI, but it was a record. In the third inning of the Cardinals April 23, 1999 game against the Dodgers at Dodger Stadium, lightening struck twice. Having never hit a grand slam before, Fernando Tatis hit two in the same inning off the same pitcher, Chan Ho Park. That feat alone and the eight RBI in a single inning set a new baseball record that will likely never be broken.

Memories and Moments

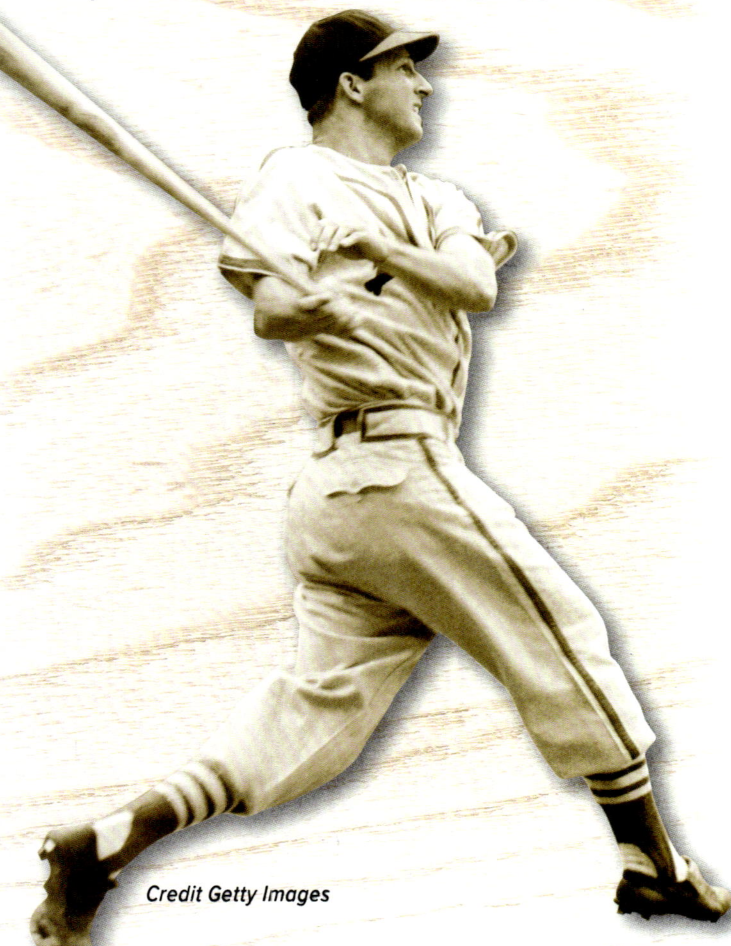
Credit Getty Images

The Final Game! It was the perfect ending for baseball's "perfect warrior." On September 29, 1963, Stan Musial, after playing in 3,025 games, played his final contest. In the sixth inning of a scoreless game at Busch Stadium, Musial came to bat and after fouling off two pitches, "the Man" lined a curveball between first and second base beyond a diving Pete Rose. It was hit number 3,630 and RBI 1,951 in his career to give the Redbirds the lead. Then it was over. Gary Kolb came out to pinch-run, while an adoring, standing-room-only crowd stood in applause as Musial trotted off the field one last time.

GENERAL ADMISSION

No 0488

St. Louis National Baseball Club, Inc.
NATIONAL LEAGUE BUSCH STADIUM

SUNDAY - DAY

SEPT. 29, 1963

RAIN CHECK

In the event 3 innings of one game are not played, except when the home team is in the lead at the end of 4 1-2 innings, this coupon will be good during Championship Season for exchange at Box Of. for this price ticket. Subject to prior sale.

Adm. 1.3619
Fed. Tax .0400
Lic. Fee .0681
St. Tax .0300
Total $1.50

President

5 Moonshots! It didn't all happen in one inning or one game, but it did happen all on one day during a doubleheader. Stan Musial became the first player in baseball history to hit five home runs in one day. On May 2, 1954, while playing the New York Giants in St. Louis, Musial slammed three homers in the first game of a doubleheader and then got two more in the nightcap. The five home runs produced nine RBI as Stan went 6-for-8, scoring six runs and collecting 22 total bases in the two Redbird wins.

At Last! Branch Rickey helped Jackie Robinson break baseball's color barrier with the Dodgers in 1947. That same year, St. Louis's other team, the Browns, signed two African Americans: Hank Thompson and Willard Brown. However, it would be another seven years before Tom Alston (right) took the field and broke the "color barrier" for the Cardinals on April 13, 1954. This franchise pioneer would stick with the Redbirds through the 1957 season and pave the way for many future African American players to make the club.

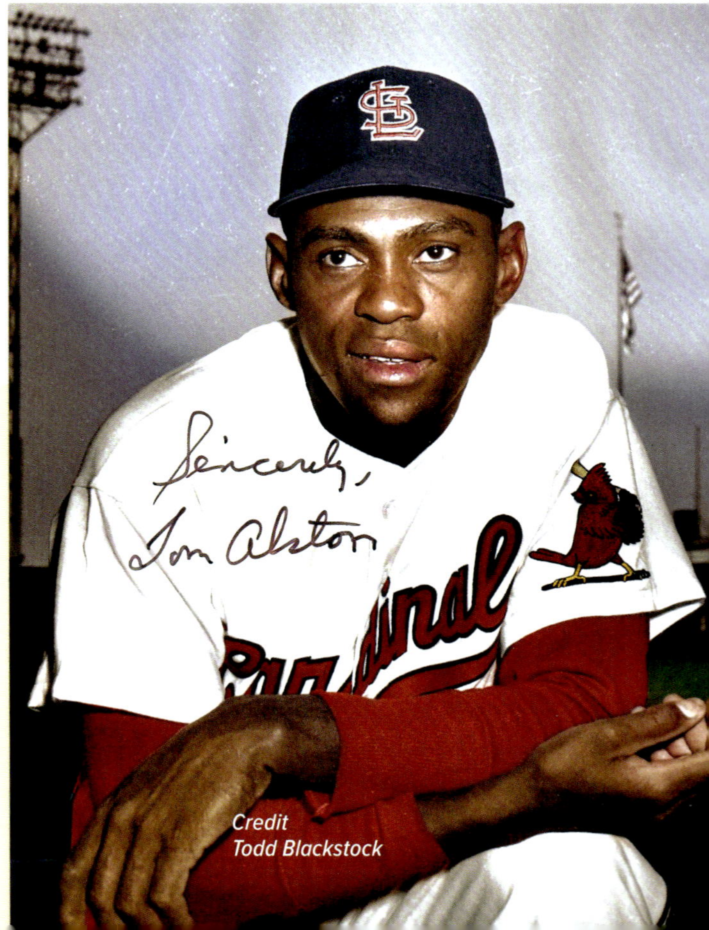

Credit
Todd Blackstock

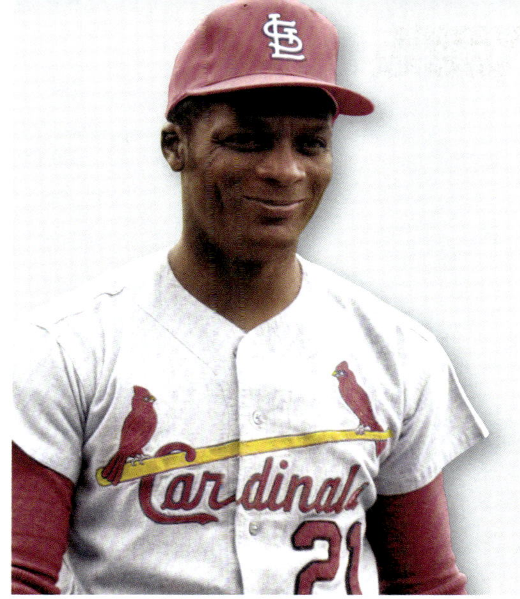

He Stood His Ground! As the expression goes, he didn't just "take one for the team," he took one for all major league ballplayers. After the 1969 season, Curt Flood, the Cardinals' star centerfielder, was traded to the Philadelphia Phillies. He refused to go. In a time in which there was no free agency, Flood argued that baseball's reserve clause was unfair and kept players beholden for life to the team for which they last played, even after they had satisfied the terms and conditions of their contracts. While the Supreme Court would eventually reject Flood's bid to become a free agent in 1971, his actions set the stage for eventual free agency in 1975.

Credit Missouri Historical Society, St. Louis

The best wasn't good enough! A players strike stopped play mid-way through the 1981 season. When the games finally resumed, the Cardinals would finish the season with the best overall record in the National League East Division and should have gone to the National League Championship playoff. They didn't, because baseball leadership inserted a playoff within each division that paired the teams with the best records before and after the strike to determine the division champion (no matter how they finished overall). The Cardinals never made it to the playoffs, but the Expos and Phillies did.

1981 OVERALL END OF SEASON RECORDS

NL EAST	WINS	LOSSES	PCT.	GB
St. Louis Cardinals	59	43	0.58	—
Montreal Expos**	60	48	0.56	2
Philadelphia Phillies*	59	48	0.55	2.5
Pittsburgh Pirates	46	56	0.45	13
New York Mets	41	62	0.40	18.5
Chicago Cubs	38	65	0.37	21.5

** Best record pre-strike   ** Best record post-strike*

Brummer's Surprise! He will never be a Hall of Famer or even be remembered as a great player, but everyone listening to the game on August 22, 1982, remembers Cardinal announcer Mike Shannon's call of the slow-footed, third-string catcher's steal of home plate in the 12th inning to win a key game in the 1982 pennant race. The catcher was Glen Brummer. He was on third base, with two outs, and a 1–2 count on David Green. Needing a run and a win, Brummer took off and surprised everyone in the stadium with a steal no one expected—a game winner!

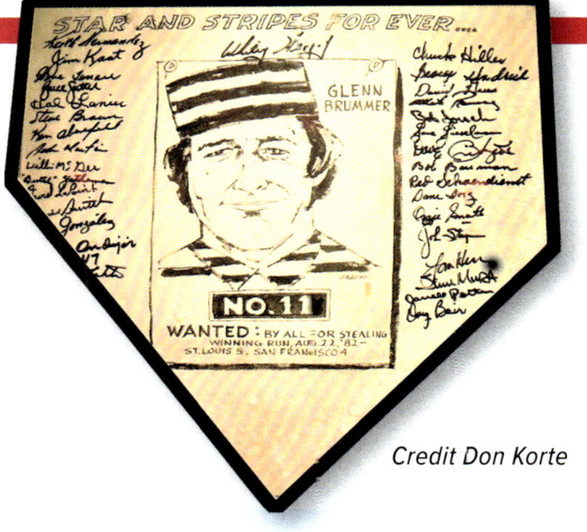

Credit Don Korte

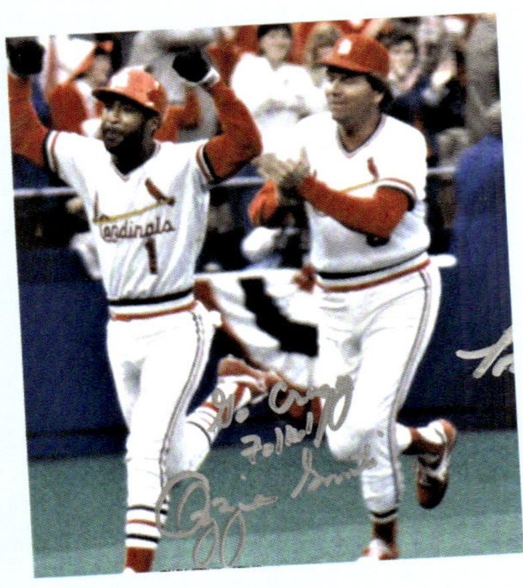

"Go crazy, folks! Go crazy!" became one of the storied exclamations of Cardinal radio announcer Jack Buck to end Game 5 of the 1985 N.L. Championship playoffs on September 14, 1985. It was a must-win game for the Cardinals, who were tied two-games apiece with the Dodgers. The next two games would be played in Los Angeles, making it harder to win. With the game tied in the bottom of the ninth and one out, Ozzie Smith came to the plate batting left-handed against Tom Niedenfuer. The switch-hitting Smith had never hit a left-handed home run in his previous 2,967 at bats in the majors—until this day. As Dodger manager Tommy Lasorda later said, "To get beat on a home run by Ozzie Smith, that's unbelievable." And it's also enough to make you "go crazy!"

Memories and Moments

The MAC Attack! Although its luster has been dimmed due to time and alleged steroid use, there was no better place to be in 1998 than watching Mark McGwire chase baseball's home run record. That summer baseball fans were abuzz following the dramatic home run race between McGwire and the Cubs' Sammy Sosa to best Roger Maris's record of 61 home runs in a season. On September 8th before a standing room only crowd inside and thousands more outside the stadium; McGwire launched a fourth-inning line drive just over the left field wall for the new record. But he didn't stop at 62; he continued swinging for the fences until he got his 70th homer on the final day of the season. Although Barry Bonds broke the record in 2001, the magic of the "summer of '98" lives on in fans' memories.

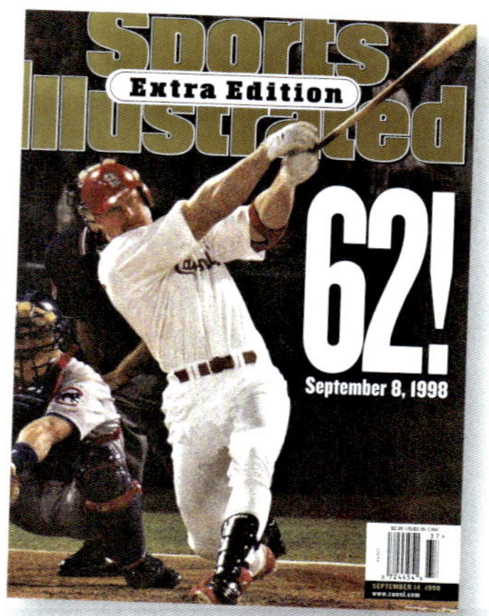

The Reunion! It had been eight seasons since Albert Pujols last walked to the plate in Busch Stadium. He had gone to Los Angeles, where he hit his 500th and 600th home runs along with his 3,000 hit. Now he was back in St. Louis in June, 2019, with the Angels, and baseball's best fans once more showed the love for their hero who gave them the best 11 seasons ever played in the history of baseball. It was a weekend of standing-room-only crowds and standing ovations. It was also a weekend with a few more home runs. It didn't matter that they were runs for the visitors. What mattered was he was back and doing what he had done so many times before, and the fans got one more opportunity to stand and cheer Albert—or so they thought.

Credit Getty Images

He's Back! Pujols returned to St. Louis in 2022. He was a Cardinal once more, and he would put together an amazing season that combined the memories of Mark McGwire's home run chase with Stan Musial's farewell. Pujols had said he would retire at season's end, but he also had some business to finish. He hoped to become only the fouth player in baseball history to hit 700 home runs. As was often the case, Albert didn't disappoint and in fact finished the season and his career with 703 home runs.

Credit Wikimedia Commons, Ryan Casey Aguinaldo

A September to Remember! Not only did Pujols say the 2022 season would be his last, it would also be the last for long-time teammate Yadier Molina. What began as a farewell tour across the majors became a year of records and a playoff chase. While Albert was chasing 700, Yadi was chasing 325—the all-time record for most starts by a major league tandem, which he would share with Adam Wainwright. On September 19th, they got it on their way to a final total of 328.

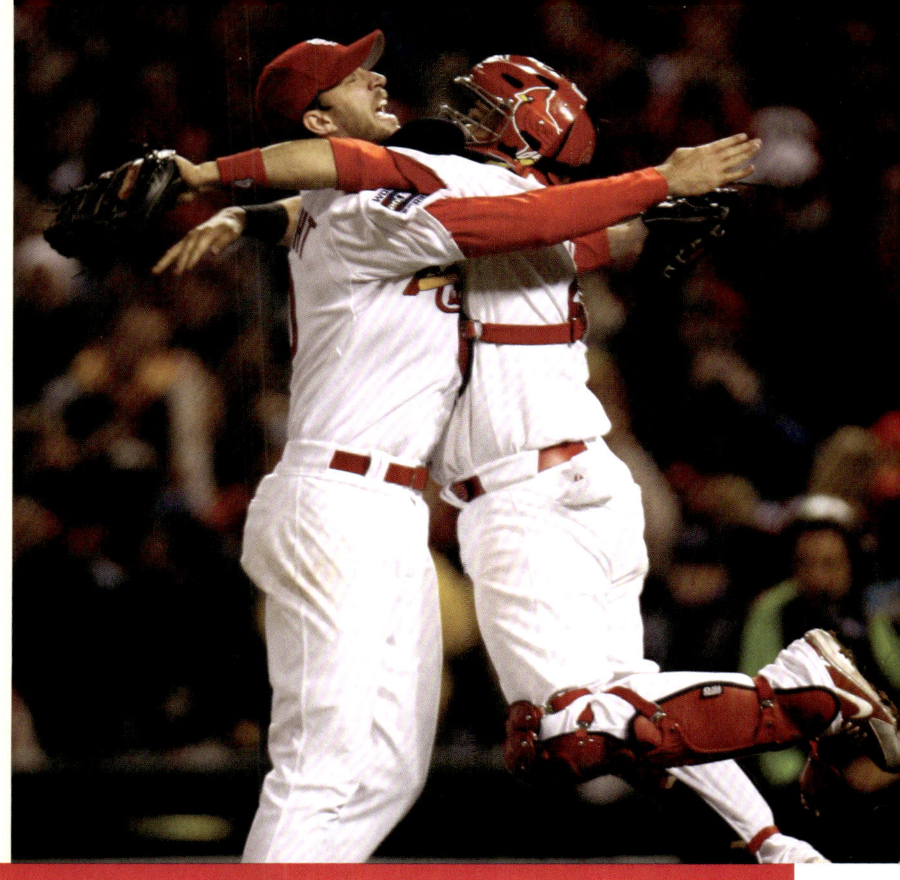

Wainwright and Molina celebrate
Credit Getty Images

The End! October 8, 2022, seemed a lot like September 29, 1963—Stan Musial's last game. The Cardinals made it to the playoffs, but it didn't end well for the team—but it wasn't because of Albert and Yadi. Facing elimination in Game 2 of the best-of-three playoffs against the Phillies, Pujols came to bat in the eighth inning hoping to rally his team from a 0–2 deficit. With a man on first base, Pujols ripped a single down the third base line for the last hit of his career—number 3,384. No runs scored, but in the ninth, and once more with a man on first base with two outs, Molina punched a single to right-center field, and like Musial, a pinch-runner came out to run and Molina took his final curtain-call before his loving fans as the careers of two of the Cardinals' best came to a close.

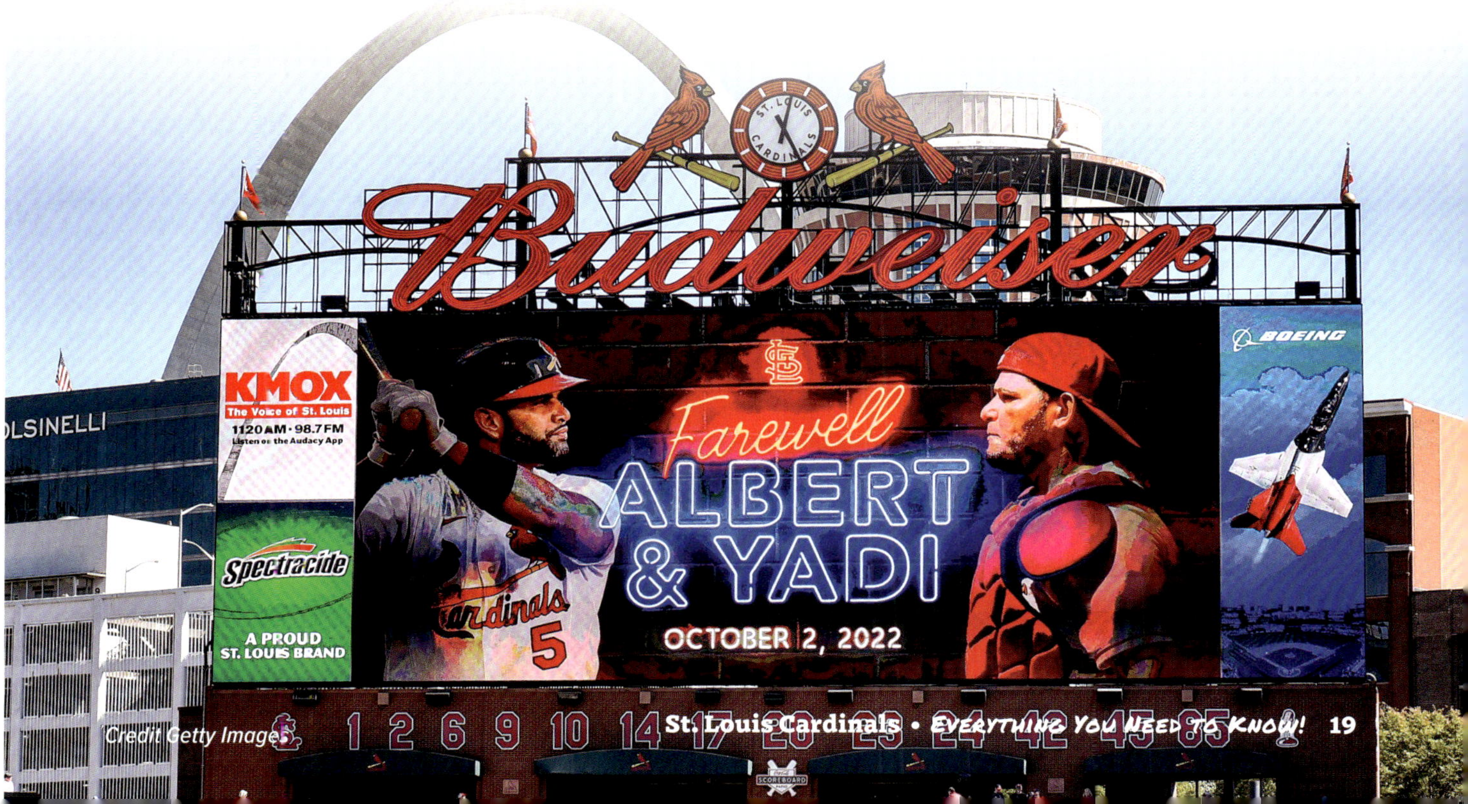

Credit Getty Images

Pitchers

Good pitching beats good hitting, or so the story goes across the world of baseball. In all of baseball history, only the Yankees (.570), Dodgers (.536), and Giants (.530) have a better winning percentage than the Cardinals' .521 posting through the 2022 season. Much of the Redbirds' success can be attributed to their strong stable of pitchers over the years.

Credit Getty Images

"Me and Paul" was the pitching cry of the Dean brothers leading up to the 1934 World Series. "Me" refers to Dizzy Dean, the colorful, larger-than-life ace of the 1930s "Gas-House Gang." On the flip side, Paul Dean, nicknamed "Daffy," was a superb pitcher who twice won 19 games (1934 and '35). But Dizzy was the best, and he would tell you so, saying: "Anybody who's ever had the privilege of seeing me play knows that I am the greatest pitcher in the world." Dizzy won baseball's MVP in 1934 after becoming the National League's last pitcher to win 30 games. Dizzy was also the MVP runner-up the following two seasons.

"Wee Willie" Bill Sherdel, the Cardinals winningest left-hander, was a key member of the World Series teams in the 1920s and early '30s. He compiled a record of 153–131 while pitching for the Redbirds (1918–30, '32). "Wee Willie's" relief pitching performance on July 20, 1924, was one of the most efficient ever. He got three outs on a single pitch. With the bases loaded, he got the Phillies' George Harper to hit into a 3–6–4 triple play!

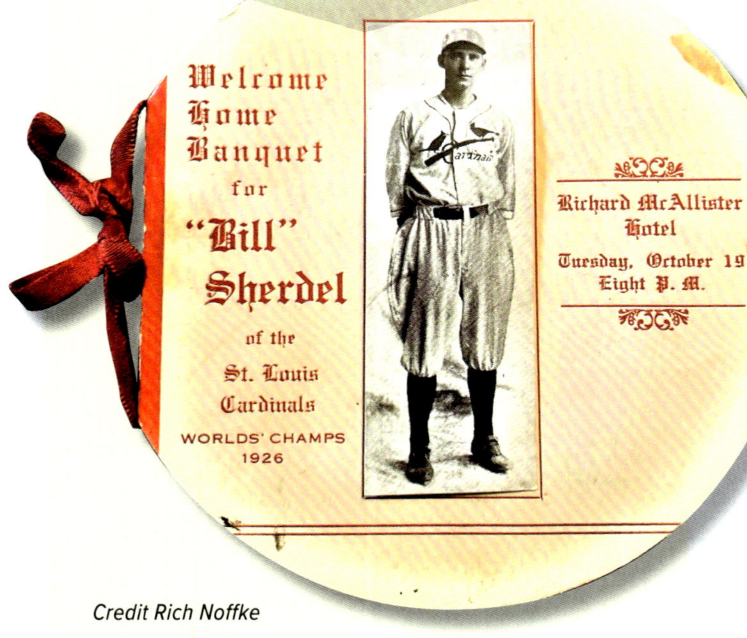

Credit Rich Noffke

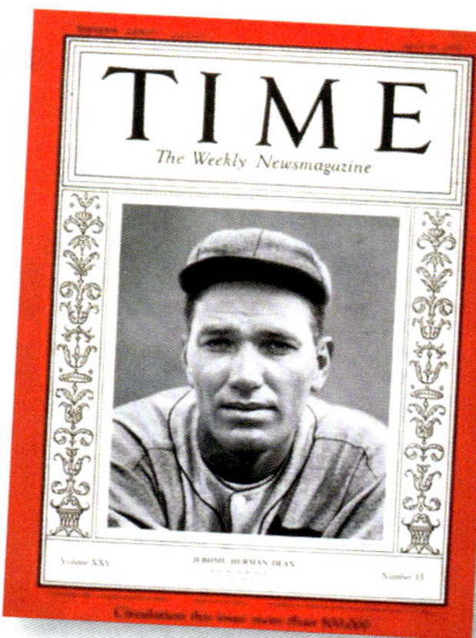

There is no better story of Dizzy always looking for the headlines than after a September 21, 1934 doubleheader. In the second game, Paul Dean threw a no-hitter against the Dodgers. "Old Diz" had thrown a three-hit shutout in the first game and said afterwards: "Shoot, if I'da known Paul was gonna pitch a no-hitter, I'da pitched me one too." On the way to that year's pennant, the brothers combined for 49 of the team's 95 wins—four more than Dizzy's preseason prediction that: "me and Paul are gonna win 45 games." In that year's Fall Classic they each picked up two victories in the win over the Tigers. Injuries shortened each brother's career, so there is no telling just how good they really could have been. In the end, Dizzy Dean talked big, but his legacy is that he always delivered big as well!

The 1950s saw another set of brothers take the mound. The McDaniel Brothers, Lindy and Von, initially looked to be the reincarnation of the Deans. Lindy McDaniel played the first eight years (1955–62) of his 21-year career with the Cardinals. He was a two-time All-Star and the winner of the first *Sporting News* Reliever of the Year Award for the National League in 1960, when relief pitching was first becoming a specialty position. Lindy would win it again in 1963 with the Cubs. After starting 4–0 in '57, Von would last only 14 more games.

Lindy and Von McDaniel
Credit Getty Images

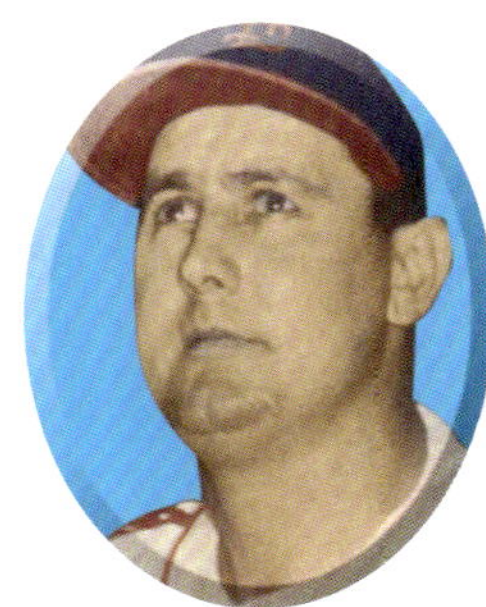

Mort Cooper
Credit St. Louis Browns Historical Society

The Cardinals had another set of famous brothers during the team's dominating years of the 1940s—pitcher Mort Cooper and his brother Walker, a catcher. Beginning in 1942 Mort would win 21 games in each of the next three seasons as the team's ace hurler. His 65–22 record over that period guided the Redbirds to three pennants (1942–44) and earned him the MVP in '42. In his eight seasons in a Cardinal uniform, Cooper was an impressive 105–50.

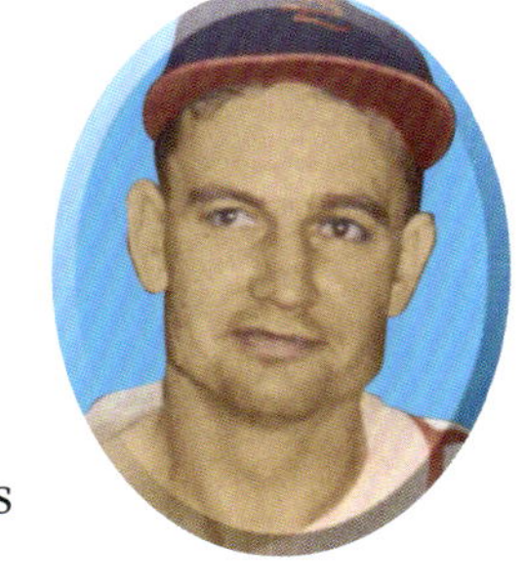

Walker Cooper
Credit St. Louis Browns Historical Society

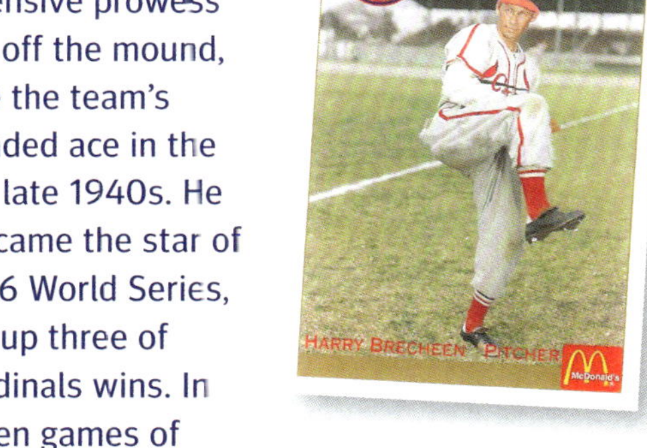

Harry Brecheen, nicknamed "the Cat" for his defensive prowess coming off the mound, became the team's left-handed ace in the mid- to late 1940s. He also became the star of the 1946 World Series, picking up three of the Cardinals wins. In the seven games of the 1943, '44, and '46 World Series that Brecheen pitched, he would record an amazing .083 ERA.

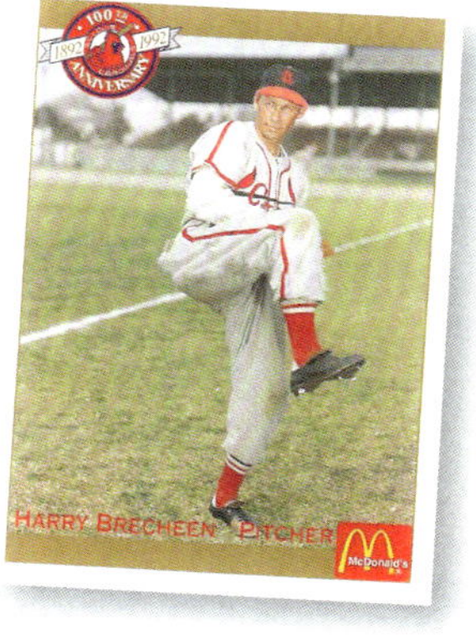

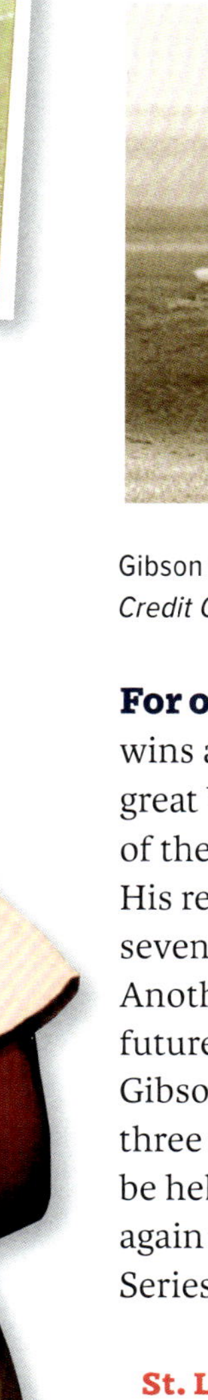

Gibby! As Von McDaniel's career flamed out, the Cardinals greatest pitcher of all-time took off. Bob Gibson made it to the big leagues in 1959. During his 17-year career (all with the Redbirds), he was an All-Star nine times. He led the team to three pennants while winning the N.L. MVP (1968), two Cy Young Awards (1968 and '70), two World Series MVPs (1964 and '67), and nine Gold Gloves. Known as perhaps the most intense competitor to ever play the game, Gibson would lead the franchise in wins, strikeouts, shutouts, games pitched and complete games on his way to the Hall of Fame.

Credit Getty Images

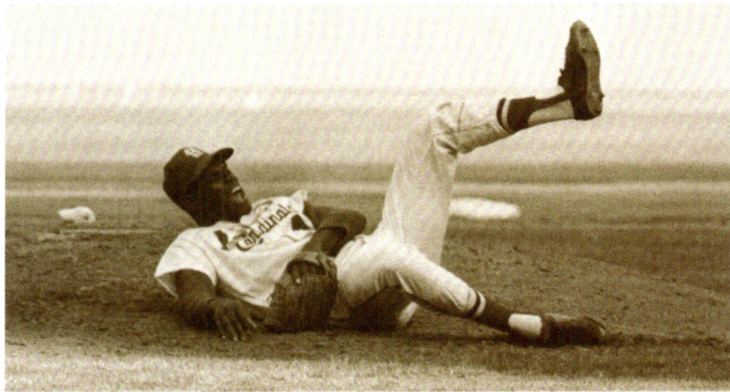

Gibson takes a Clemente line drive to his leg.
Credit Getty Images

For over a decade (1963–72) Gibson would average 19 wins and 200 strikeouts per season. In 1974, he joined the great Walter Johnson as the only pitcher in the history of the game, up to that time, to strike out 3,000 batters. His record-setting 17-strikeout Series game and string of seven consecutive World Series wins was simply amazing. Another remarkable moment occurred in July 1967, when future Hall of Famer Roberto Clemente shot a line drive off Gibson's right leg for a single. Gibson got up and pitched to three more batters before his fibula snapped and he had to be helped off the field. He would recover in time to pitch again in September and lead the team to their eighth World Series championship.

Pitchers

Nellie Briles may have been the real MVP for the Cardinals in 1967. When Gibson went down, Briles stepped up. He was 4–3 when Gibson got hurt, and he wound up 14–5 by season's end, including nine straight wins and then a win in Game 3 of the 1967 World Series. Could the Cardinals have been world champions without Briles?

Credit State Historical Society of Missouri

John Tudor was 63–26 with the club (1985–88, '90), but his 1985 performance not only got the team to the World Series, it is one of the best seasons in baseball history. After being traded to the Cardinals from Pittsburgh to start the 1985 season, Tudor began the season 1–7. Then Tudor's high school catcher noticed a hitch in his delivery while watching him on television. Tudor made the fix and then began a 20–1 stretch with a 1.37 ERA that propelled the Cardinals to the 1985 World Series. Tudor won his first two Series starts before losing the Game 7 finale.

Credit Getty Images

Chris Carpenter *(below)* **and Adam Wainwright** became a formidable tandem of the Cardinals teams of the 2000s. Carpenter came to the Cardinals as damaged goods from the Toronto Blue Jays in 2002. The Redbirds let him heal into 2004. Carpenter then became their ace on two championship-winning teams (2006 and '11), a three-time All-Star (2005, '06, and '10), and the winner of the 2005 National League Cy Young Award. Always a competitor, Carpenter was 3–0 in his four World Series games.

Steve Carlton would pick up 77 of his 329 wins as a Cardinal beginning in 1965, during the first seven seasons of his 24-year Hall of Fame career. He would pitch in three games of the 1967–68 World Series and represent the Redbirds in three All-Star games (1968–69, '71) before being traded to the Phillies just before the 1972 season. His biggest game as a Cardinal was his 19-strikeout performance (a new record) against the Mets on September 15, 1969.

Credit Getty Images

Joaquin Andujar doesn't show up on the franchise's leader board, but he was the ace of the 1982 and '85 pennant-winning teams. The four-time All-Star spent five seasons with the Redbirds going 68—53. He won both of his starts in the 1982 Series, including the clinching Game 7. He would help the Redbirds win the 1985 pennant, but he did not get a win in either of his two appearances in the Series.

Credit Getty Images

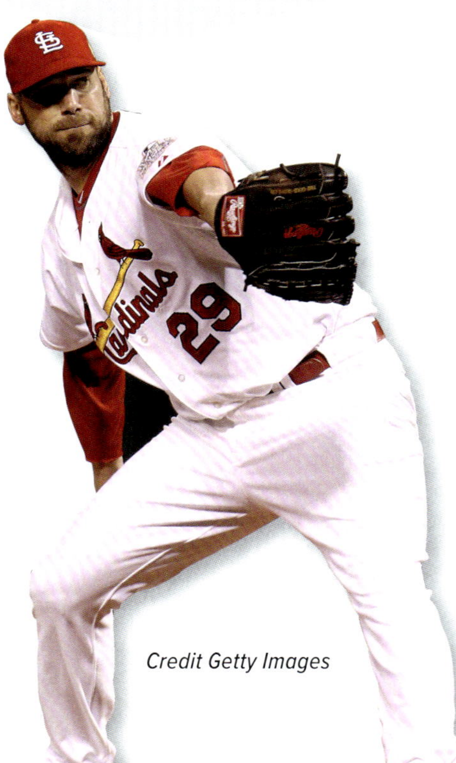

Credit Getty Images

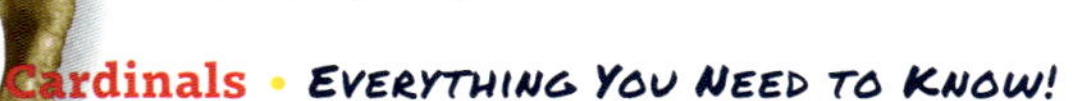

Adam Wainwright has spent all 18 years of his big league career with the Cardinals (2005–23). He started out as one of baseball's best relievers and transitioned into one of the game's best starters. With an overwhelming curveball nicknamed "Uncle Charlie," Wainwright is remembered for throwing the pitches for the last outs in the 2006 National League Championship game against Carlos Beltran and the 2006 World Series against Brandon Inge—both were called out looking! He missed the 2011 Series due to injuries, and in 2013 he took two losses in that year's Fall Classic. Always a gamer, the three-time All-Star and two-time National League wins leader not only ranks high on the Cardinals pitching leader board, but he and batterymate Yadier Molina own the all-time record for most starts by a major league tandem.

Credit Getty Images

Todd Worrell spent six years of his 11-year career with the Cardinals. He won the 1986 Rookie of the Year Award solely on his performance as a relief pitcher. Like Sutter, Worrell would never start a game in the Majors. He collected 129 of his 256 career saves as a Cardinal. In 1986, Worrell led the league in saves while winning the N.L.'s Rolaids Relief Award. He also represented the Redbirds in the 1988 All-Star game.

Lee Smith joined the Cardinals in 1990 after Worrell got hurt and recorded 160 of his 478 career saves during the next four years of his 18-year Hall of Fame career. Smith's two best years with the Cardinals were 1991 and '92, when he led the league in saves (47 and 43) while winning the Rolaids Relief Man Award each year. He was an All-Star three times with the Cardinals (1991–93).

Credit Getty Images

Since Lindy McDaniel claimed the first "Fireman of the Year" award in 1960, relief pitching has become an integral part of the game. Bruce Sutter won the award three times (1981–82, 84) while collecting 127 of his 300 career saves during his four seasons with the Redbirds (1981–'84). No save was more memorable than his Game 7 save of the 1982 World Series, which triggered Jack Buck to declare: "and that's a World Series winner!"

Credit Getty Images

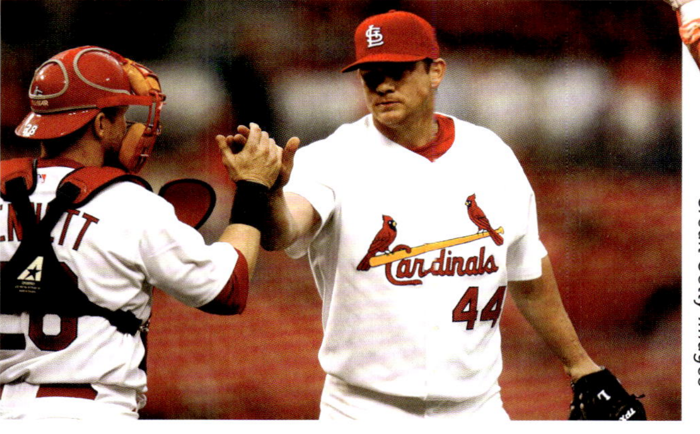

Credit Getty Images

After playing for the Mets and Athletics, Jason Isringhausen came to the Cardinals in 2002. He would spend seven seasons of his 16-season career on the two Busch Stadium mounds, becoming the franchise leader in saves. He would record 217 of his 300 career saves with the Redbirds while leading the league in saves in 2004 and representing the team in the 2005 All-Star Game.

Infielders

Good hitting combined with good fielding has been a winning combination for Cardinal players over the years. A look at the franchise's leading hitters across the infield, outfield, and behind the plate reveals a who's who of baseball's greatest players. Many would play their way into the hallowed halls of the National Baseball Hall of Fame.

"Hornsby is the greatest hitter I've ever had to face. I've tried to fool him every way possible, but it just cannot be done. Personally, I don't think a more skillful man ever stepped up to the plate."
—HALL OF FAME PITCHER GROVER CLEVELAND ALEXANDER

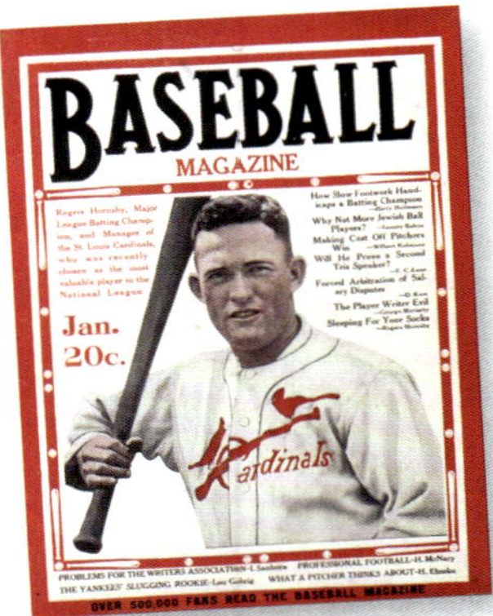

Credit Getty Images

One of Rogers Hornsby's two National League MVP selections came as a Cardinal (1925). Twice while with the Redbirds, Hornsby won baseball's Triple Crown (1922 and '25) by leading the league in batting average, home runs, and RBIs. For six straight seasons as a Cardinal (1920–25) he led the league in hitting. In three of those seasons he hit over .400—the last player to do so in the N.L. Twice he led the league in homers, and four times he led the league in RBI. He was recognized as the greatest right-handed hitter of all time when he retired with a .378 batting average—that is, until another Cardinal came along.

Jim Bottomley spent the first 11 seasons of his 16-year Hall of Fame career with the Cardinals (1922–32). He played on the first four Cardinal pennant winners. While his hitting prowess was often overshadowed by teammate Rogers Hornsby's stats, Bottomley won the MVP during the 1928 pennant-winning season. That same year he led the league in home runs and RBI. Ironically his other RBI title came in another pennant winning year—1926.

That Cardinal was Albert Pujols. Used primarily as a first baseman, Pujols joined the Redbirds in 2001 and put on a show never before seen in baseball. For the first 11 seasons of his career he was simply "a machine." Between 2001 and 2011, Pujols was the most dominant player in the game. It was like he was programmed to produce, and produce he did. During this 11-year period, Pujols led the majors with 445 homers (the most in history), 455 doubles (tied most in history), 1,291 runs scored (most in history), 915 extra-base hits (most in history), 3,893 total bases (most in history) and a 1,037 OPS (second only to Barry Bonds). With so many stats noted "most in history" for an 11-year period, it means Hall of Famers like Aaron, Cobb, Ruth, and Williams weren't any better. Albert was hands-down the best. He was a no-brainer for Rookie of the Year in 2001 and would be an All-Star in nine of those first 11 years. He would also go to the mid-season classic when he returned for his amazing finale in 2022. Pujols won the MVP title three times (2005, '08, and '09). He would lead the league in hitting in 2003 and home runs in 2009 and 2010. By the end of his career, Pujols had hit 703 home runs—something only three other players had accomplished. In baseball history, his 2,218 RBI and 6,211 total bases are second only to Hank Aaron. His 3,384 hits are the ninth most in the history of the game. But it wasn't all about producing at the plate. He produced in the field as well, winning Gold Gloves in 2006 and 2010. Albert Pujols began his career like a programed machine and wound up as one of baseball's best ever.

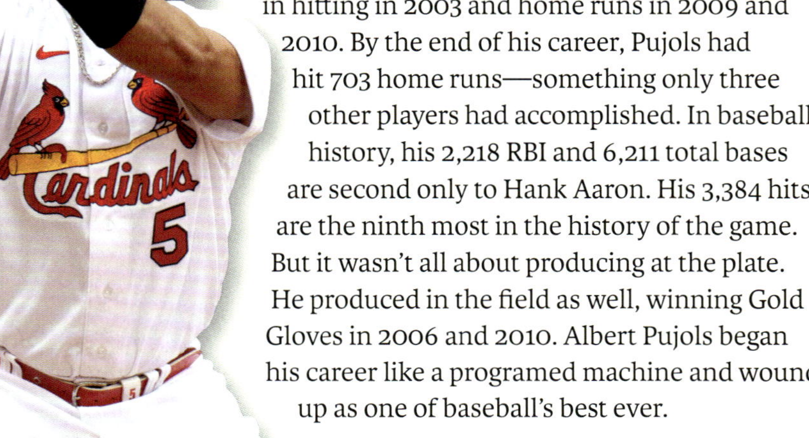

Credit Getty Images

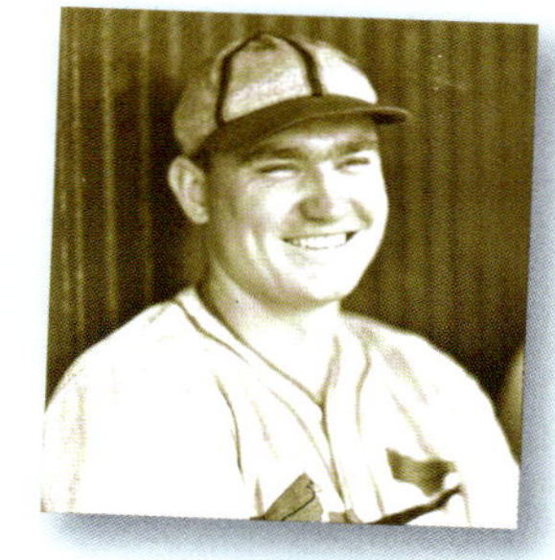

Johnny Mize got the nickname “the Big Cat” for his smooth fielding at first base. The first six seasons of his 15-year Hall of Fame career were spent with the Cardinals (1936–41), which meant despite his greatness, he never won a pennant as a Redbird. Besides his defense, Mize was a great hitter. As a Cardinal he would go to the All-Star game four times. Mize won the 1939 batting title, two home run titles (1939–40), and one RBI title (1940). Of his 359 home runs, 158 were hit in a Cardinal uniform.

Orlando Cepeda won two pennants with the Redbirds. The San Francisco Giants traded their former Rookie of the Year to the Cardinals in a mid-season deal for Ray Sadecki in 1966. Cepeda delivered an MVP season in 1967 as the Redbirds won the World Series, and he helped his team to another pennant the next year. But his declining play led the Cardinals to trade him to the Atlanta Braves in 1969 in exchange for Joe Torre.

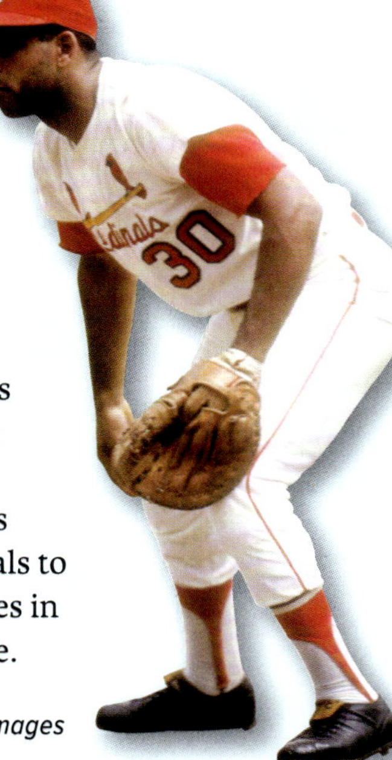

Credit Getty Images

Mark McGwire came to the Cardinals from the Oakland A’s at the trade deadline of 1997. With the A’s he had been selected Rookie of the Year and made 9 trips to the All-Star Game. Twice he had been baseball’s home run leader. It seems, however, he was just warming up for the final seasons of his career with the Redbirds. McGwire was the baseball home run leader 2 times while wearing the “birds on the bat” and also a 3-time All-Star. While the steroid scandal has likely cost McGwire a plaque in the Hall of Fame, he still holds baseball’s career record for hitting a home run every 10.6 at bats.

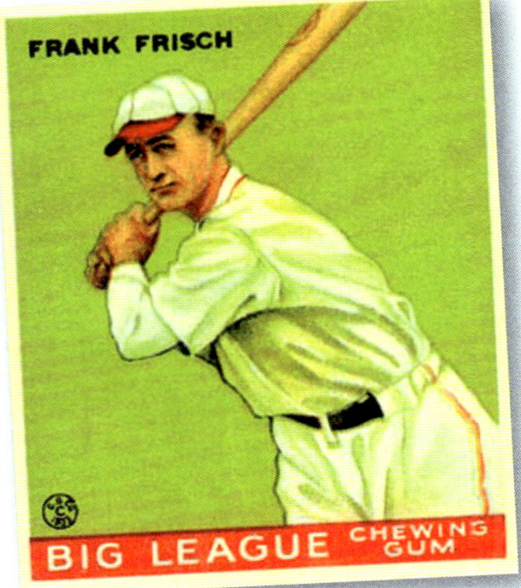

Credit Wikimedia Commons

Keith Hernandez is remembered as a slick-fielding first baseman who spent 10 of his 17 seasons with the Cardinals. A key member of the 1982 World Series team and twice an All-Star with the Redbirds (1979–80), he won six of his 11 Gold Gloves in St. Louis (1978–83), along with the 1979 batting title (.344) and a share of that year’s MVP Award with Willie Stargell.

Frankie Frisch was a Hall of Fame second baseman who spent 11 of his 19 seasons with the Cardinals. Frisch came to the Cardinals in a trade for Rogers Hornsby after Hornsby had led the Redbirds to the World Championship. An MVP in 1931, Frisch was named to the first three All-Star Games ever played (1933–35). More importantly, he was one of the offensive keys for the pennant winning teams of 1928, ’30–31, and ’34. Frisch was also an early league leader in a stat that Cardinal players would soon regularly lead—stolen bases. Twice he led the N.L. in steals (1927 and ’31).

Infielders

Another Hall of Famer was known as "the redhead," but his real name was Albert "Red" Schoendienst. He spent 15 of his 19 Hall of Fame seasons as a player in a Cardinal uniform. Adding time as a manager and coach, he would wear the birds on the bat for over 60 years. Schoendienst joined the Redbirds in 1945 and was a key part of the 1946 World Championship team. He represented the Cardinals nine times in the All-Star game, winning the 1950 mid-season classic with a game-winning home run in the 14th inning.

At shortstop, the Cardinals have had two of the best to ever play the game. Marty Marion anchored the infield during the team's dominating run of the 1940s. Known in his day as "Mr. Shortstop," Marion was a better-than-average hitter, and as a lanky shortstop he seemed to get to more balls than most others. They say his long arms looked like tentacles, which led to sportswriters calling him "the Octopus." In 1944 he became the first N.L. shortstop ever to win an MVP Award and was part of four pennant-winning teams. Marion would spend all 13 years of his career in St. Louis—the first 11 with the Cardinals and the other two with the Browns.

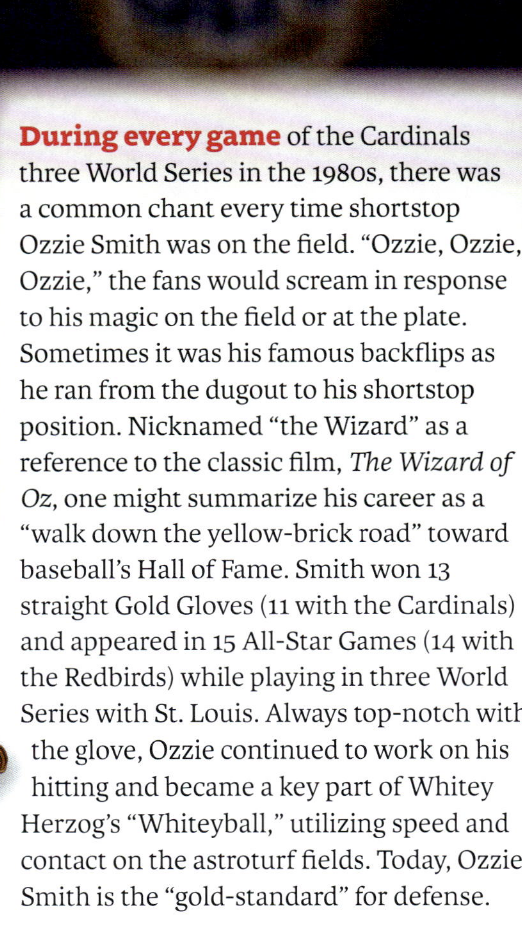

During every game of the Cardinals three World Series in the 1980s, there was a common chant every time shortstop Ozzie Smith was on the field. "Ozzie, Ozzie, Ozzie," the fans would scream in response to his magic on the field or at the plate. Sometimes it was his famous backflips as he ran from the dugout to his shortstop position. Nicknamed "the Wizard" as a reference to the classic film, *The Wizard of Oz*, one might summarize his career as a "walk down the yellow-brick road" toward baseball's Hall of Fame. Smith won 13 straight Gold Gloves (11 with the Cardinals) and appeared in 15 All-Star Games (14 with the Redbirds) while playing in three World Series with St. Louis. Always top-notch with the glove, Ozzie continued to work on his hitting and became a key part of Whitey Herzog's "Whiteyball," utilizing speed and contact on the astroturf fields. Today, Ozzie Smith is the "gold-standard" for defense.

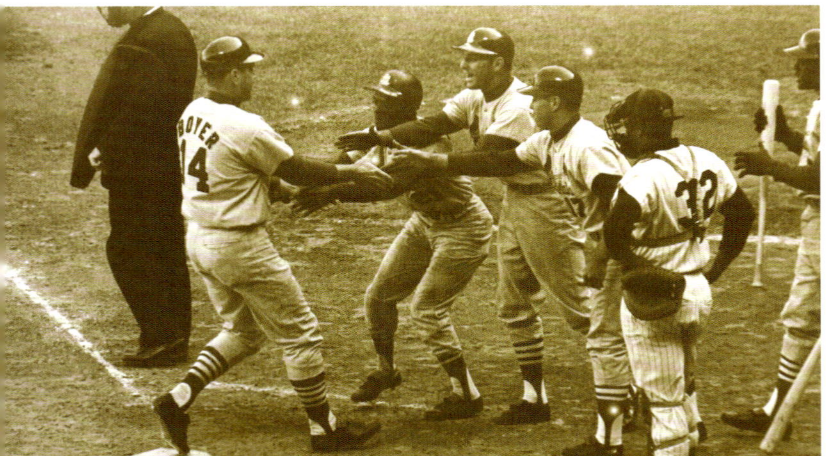

Ken Boyer spent 11 of his 15 big league seasons in St. Louis, hitting 255 of his 282 home runs as a Redbird. An 11-time All-Star, he won five Gold Gloves. Boyer's greatest season was 1964, when he won the N.L. MVP to lead the Cardinals to their first pennant in 18 seasons. His Game 4 grand slam has been called the turning point of the World Series, which saw Boyer and the Redbirds defeat his brother Clete's New York Yankees.

All images on this page credit Getty Images

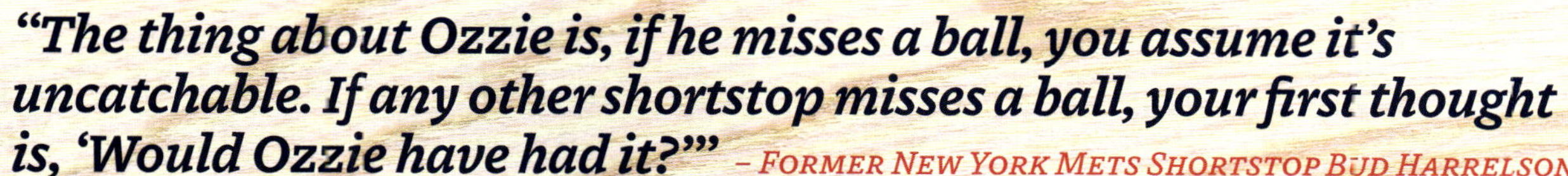

"The thing about Ozzie is, if he misses a ball, you assume it's uncatchable. If any other shortstop misses a ball, your first thought is, 'Would Ozzie have had it?'" – Former New York Mets Shortstop Bud Harrelson

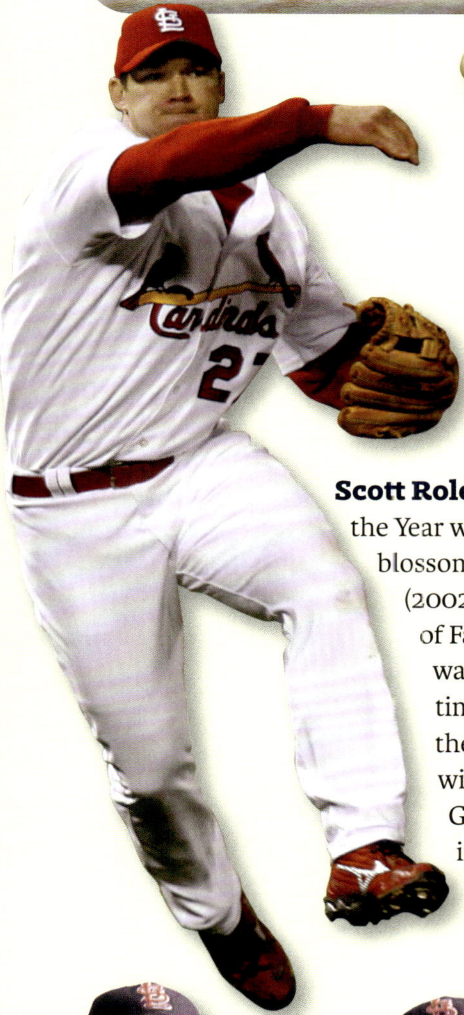

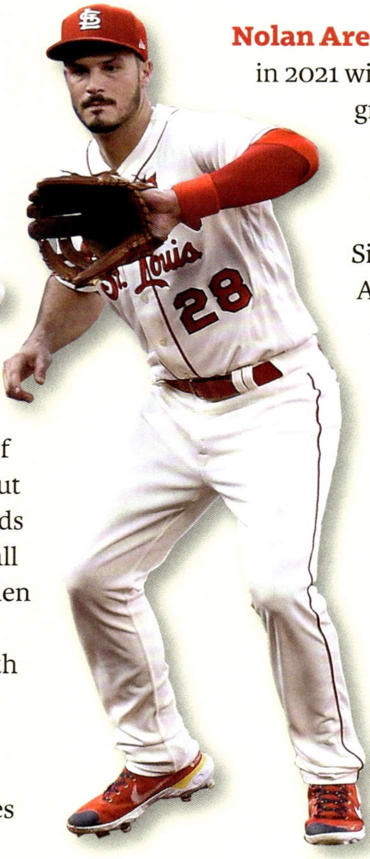

Nolan Arenado came to the Cardinals in 2021 with a reputation for defensive greatness. In Colorado, he had been a five-time All-Star while winning a Gold Glove every year since his debut in 2013. Since coming to the Redbirds, Arenado has also been an All-Star and Gold Glove winner every year. His 10 Gold Gloves ties Ichiro Suzuki for the most consecutive awards starting a big league career. He has won the Platinum Award, given to the best defender in each league every year since 2017. And Arenado can hit. He led the N.L. in home runs three times and RBIs twice as a Rockie. While the Cardinals' Busch Stadium is a different ballpark, Arenado has shown he can deliver as a Cardinal, now and in the future.

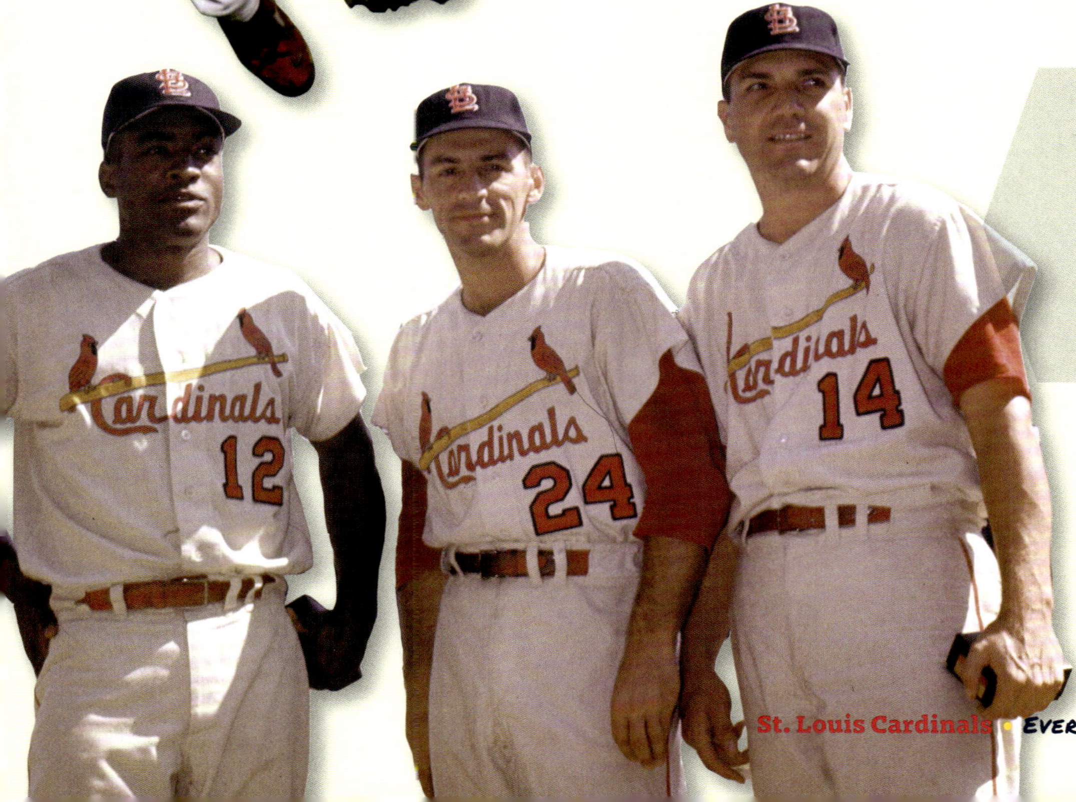

Scott Rolen was a Rookie of the Year with the Phillies, but blossomed on the Redbirds (2002–07). A recent Hall of Fame inductee, Rolen was an All-Star five times (2002–06) with the Cardinals while winning four Gold Gloves and playing in two World Series (2004, '06).

Sometimes infield greatness is not just one player but the team. The 1963 Cardinals were a prime example. Infielders Bill White (1B), Julian Javier (2B), Dick Groat (SS), and Ken Boyer (3B) were the starting infield for that year's All-Star game.

The Cardinals have definitely had an infield history of "good hit, good glove!"

Bill White, Dick Groat, and Ken Boyer
All images on this page credit Getty Images

Outfielders

An outfielder's job (besides hitting) is to run and catch fly balls or grab grounders through the infield and prevent runners from taking extra bases. The position requires speed and a good arm. While having a history of good outfielders, the Cardinals also had one of the greatest players of all time patrolling the outfield at Sportsman's Park.

The greatness of Hornsby and Pujols cannot be denied, and no disrespect is meant to these two Cardinals in the statement that Stan Musial was "the greatest Cardinal of them all." Signed as a pitcher, Musial was found to be a better hitter than a pitcher. Often playing first base early in his career, Musial played the majority of his games in the outfield. As the feared Cardinal hitter would come to the plate in Brooklyn's Ebbetts Field, Dodger fans would holler, "here comes the man." They didn't say "that man," it was "the man" out of respect for one of baseball's greatest sluggers.

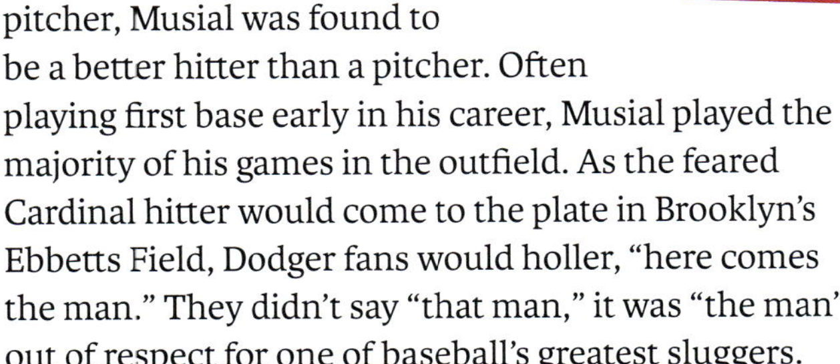

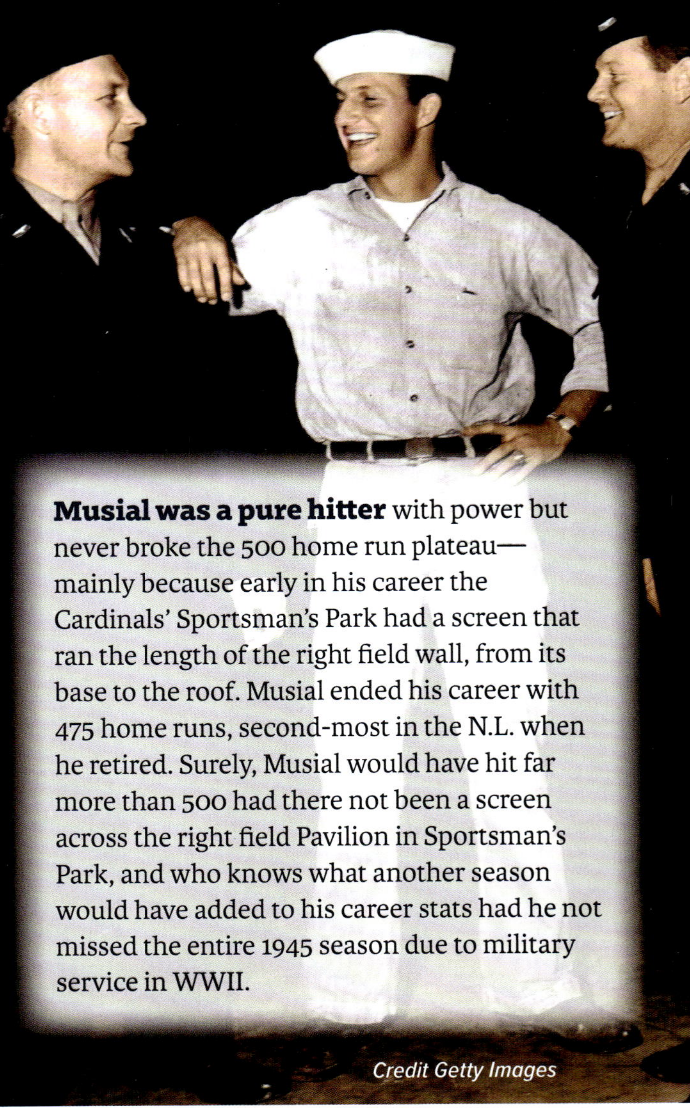

Musial was a pure hitter with power but never broke the 500 home run plateau—mainly because early in his career the Cardinals' Sportsman's Park had a screen that ran the length of the right field wall, from its base to the roof. Musial ended his career with 475 home runs, second-most in the N.L. when he retired. Surely, Musial would have hit far more than 500 had there not been a screen across the right field Pavilion in Sportsman's Park, and who knows what another season would have added to his career stats had he not missed the entire 1945 season due to military service in WWII.

Credit Getty Images

"No man has ever been a perfect ballplayer. Stan Musial, however, is the closest to being perfect in the game today... He plays as hard when his club is way out in front of a game as he does when they're just a run or two behind."

– Hall of Famer Ty Cobb

And what stats Musial had: appearances in 24 All-Star Games and four World Series, seven National League batting titles (1943, '46, '48, '50–52, and '57), and two league RBI titles. Musial was a three-time MVP (1943, '46, and '48). The word most used about Musial's career is "perfect." In 1948, he almost was. He led the league in every category (batting average, hits, doubles, triples, runs, and RBI) but missed the home run title and the Triple Crown by one dinger. He actually hit one more home run that season, but it didn't count because the game was called due to rain. But consistency was his other mark. Musial would get 3,630 hits in his career. Half of those hits (1,815) were on the road, and the other half (1,815) were at home.

Speaking of perfection, in 1887 (six seasons before the American Association Brown Stockings joined the National League), outfielder "Tip" O'Neill won the Triple Crown with a .437 batting average, 14 home runs, and 123 RBI. He also led the league in hits, doubles, triples, and runs scored, meaning he led the league in every major hitting category.

Tip O'Neill
Credit Wikimedia Commons

Enos Slaughter was the right fielder for the Cardinals great teams of the 1940s. Like many players during the war years, Slaughter spent three of his prime baseball years (1943–1945) not playing ball due to WWII. He would return from the war in 1946 and with his “Mad Dash,” won the Redbirds a world championship. He spent 13 of his 19 years in the big leagues with the Cardinals beginning in 1938. On April 11, 1954, he was the team captain, a 10-time All Star who held the team records for games played (1,820) and RBI (1,148). He so much loved the Cardinals that when he heard the news of his trade to the New York Yankees that day, Slaughter sat at his locker and cried. When he met Stan Musial out in the parking lot of the stadium, they both cried together. Slaughter loved the Cardinals so much that upon his death in 2002, the Hall of Famer was buried in his Cardinal uniform.

Credit Getty Images

Before he finished his Hall of Fame career, Brock would hold the major league records for most bases stolen in a single season and a career. Eventually Ricky Henderson would break Lou’s marks, but it was Brock who paved the way for him and others who brought speed and excitement to the ballpark. In total, Brock helped the team to two world championships (1964 and ’67) and another pennant in ’68. He would be a six-time All-Star and an eight-time stolen base leader while pounding out 3.023 hits over 19 seasons (16 with the Cardinals).

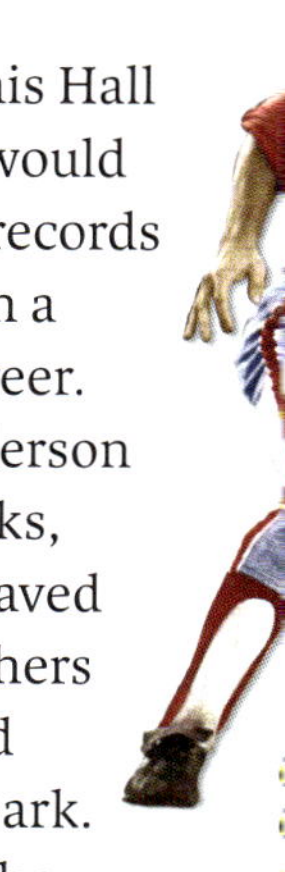

Credit Getty Images

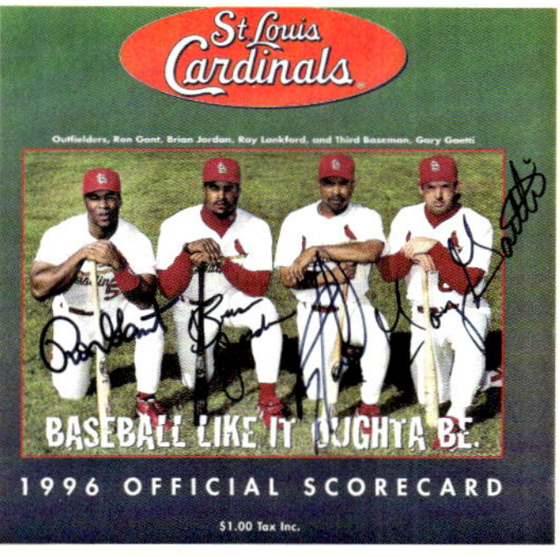

Like the other position players, outfielders have been a big part of the Cardinals winning way, and there are other standout players who have stood out in the green pastured outfields as St. Louis Cardinals.

The Cardinals’ trade with the Cubs in mid-season 1964 for Lou Brock has been ranked as one of the greatest of all times—especially for the Redbirds. St. Louis traded star pitcher Ernie Broglio for a very young and raw Brock. Lou’s hitting (.348) and base stealing (33) turned the Cardinals around in 1964 and helped the team win a championship. He soon turned the game of baseball around with his speed.

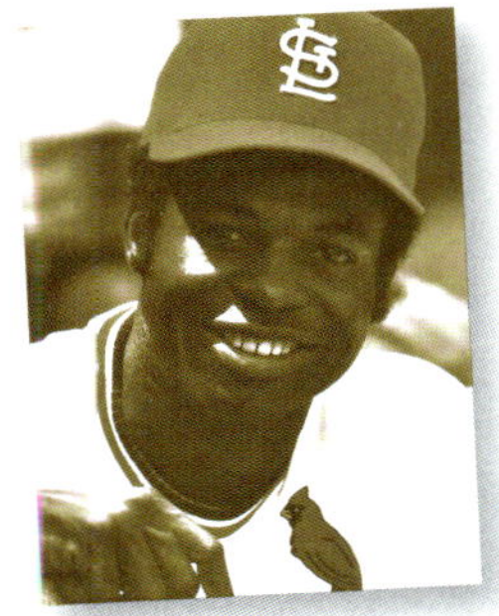

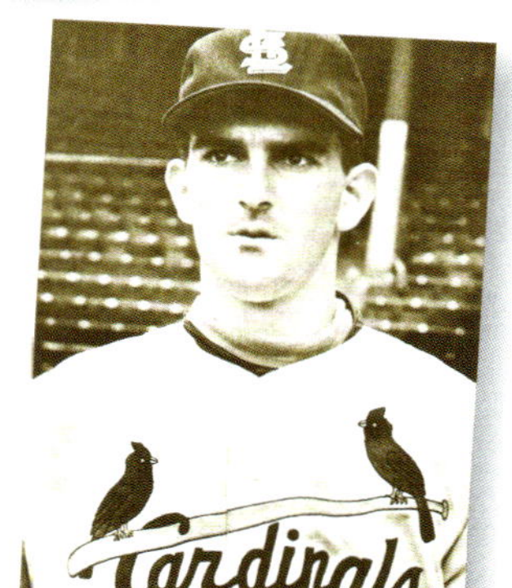

Joe Medwick was the offensive spark plug of the “Gashouse Gang.” He was a Cardinal left fielder for 11 of his 17 Hall of Fame seasons. Always a great hitter, Medwick retired with a .324 batting average. In six of his 10 All-Star appearances he would wear a Cardinal uniform. In 1937, Medwick won the MVP Award when he became the last player in the N. L. to win the Triple Crown.

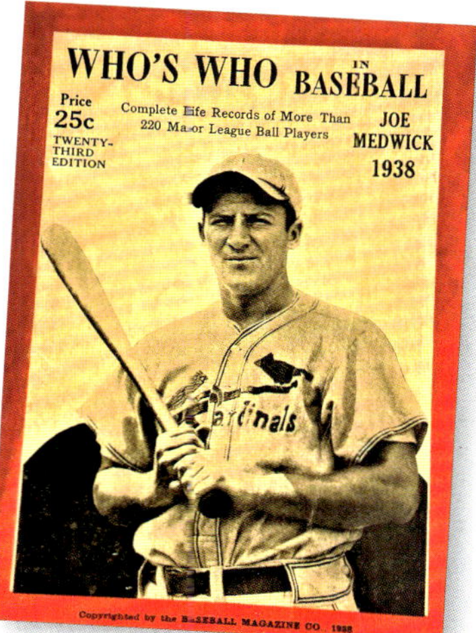

Outfielders

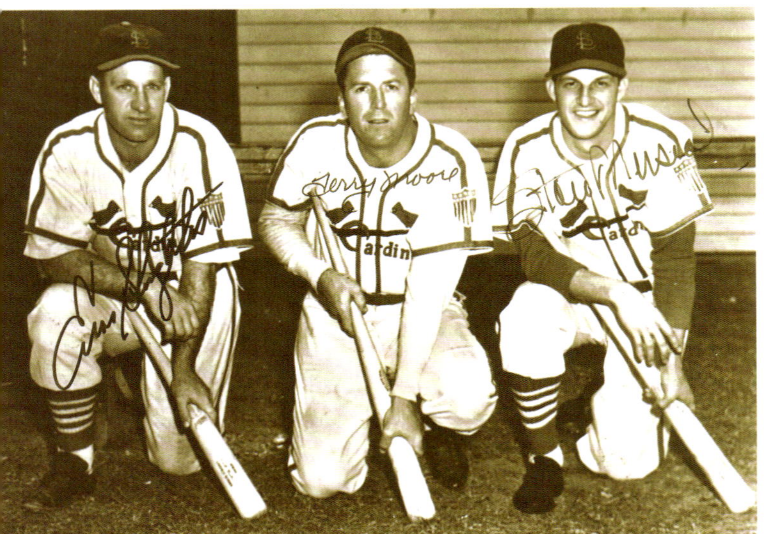

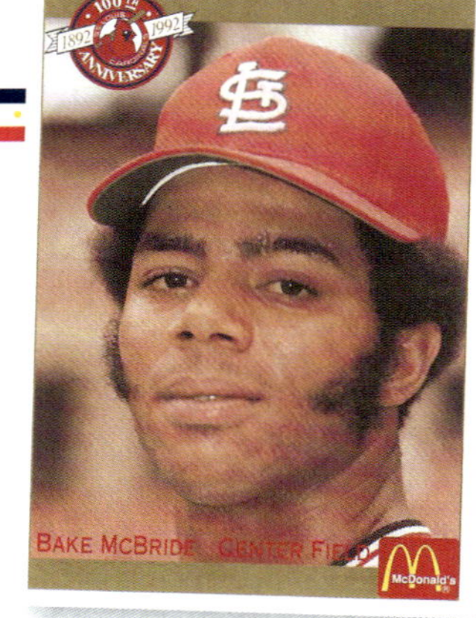

In 1974, Bake McBride became the third Cardinal outfielder to win the Rookie of the Year. He spent the first five seasons of his 11-season career with the Cardinals. Growing up in Calloway County, Missouri, McBride became known as "the Calloway Kid" as he complemented Lou Brock's hitting and base-stealing prowess in the mid-'70s. His play earned him a spot on the 1976 All-Star Team as a Cardinal before he was traded in 1977 to the Phillies.

Terry Moore's 11-year career was spent entirely with the Cardinals. It started during the heyday of the "Gashouse Gang" and went through the Cardinal championships of the 1940s. Like Slaughter, Moore lost three years to WWII (1943–45). He is best remembered as the center fielder between Musial and Slaughter during those great 1940s teams known as "the Swifties." Moore was one of the best defensive center fielders in the game and would likely have captured many Gold Glove Awards, but the first award would not be given out until 1957.

As the team's leadoff hitter, Vince Coleman was an instant spark plug with his bat and legs. He was unanimously chosen as the 1985 Rookie of the year when he stole 110 bases and would go on to lead the league in stolen bases six years in a row (1985–1990).

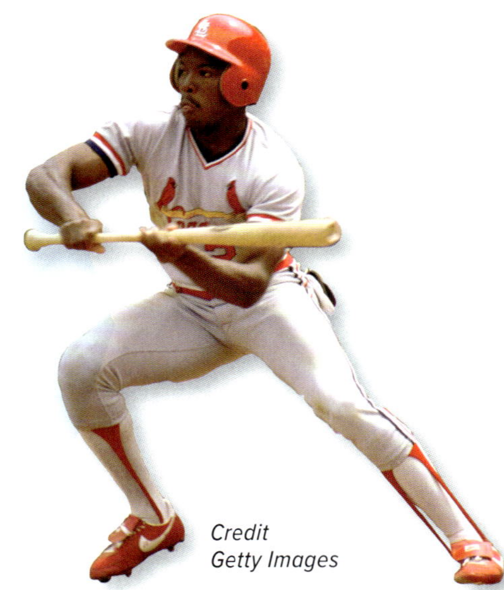

Credit Getty Images

Mike Shannon was the right fielder on the 1964 Championship team. To make room for Roger Maris, Shannon unselfishly agreed to move to third base in 1967, where he helped solidify the infield. After his retirement in 1970, Shannon moved up to the broadcast booth to announce Cardinals baseball for over 50 years.

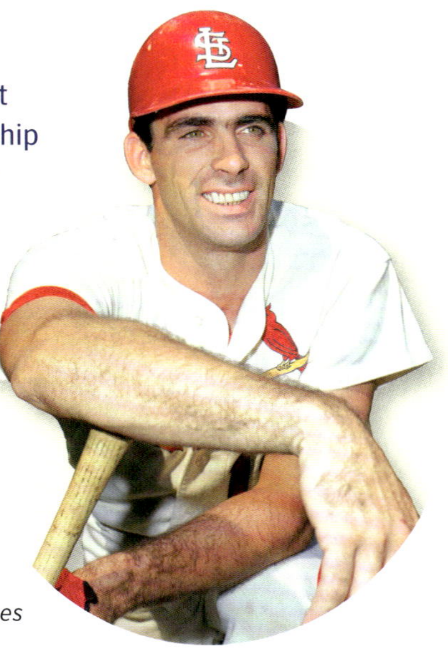

Credit Getty Images

Flood, Maris, Cepeda, and Brock
Credit Getty Images

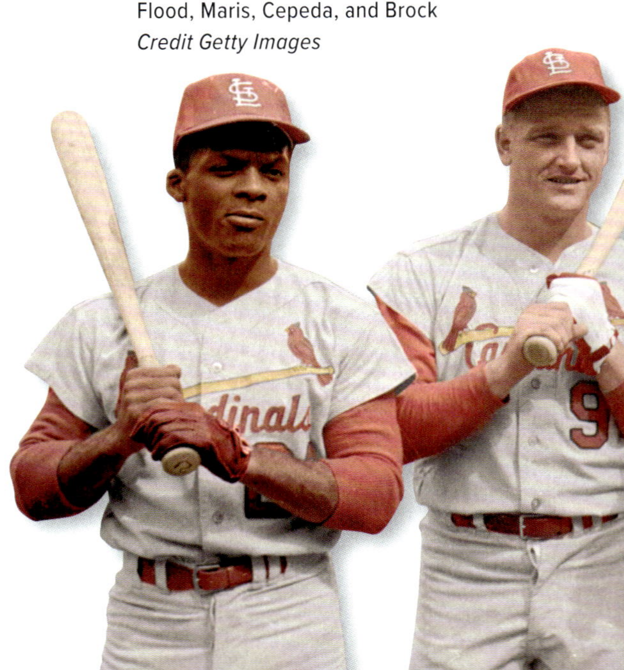

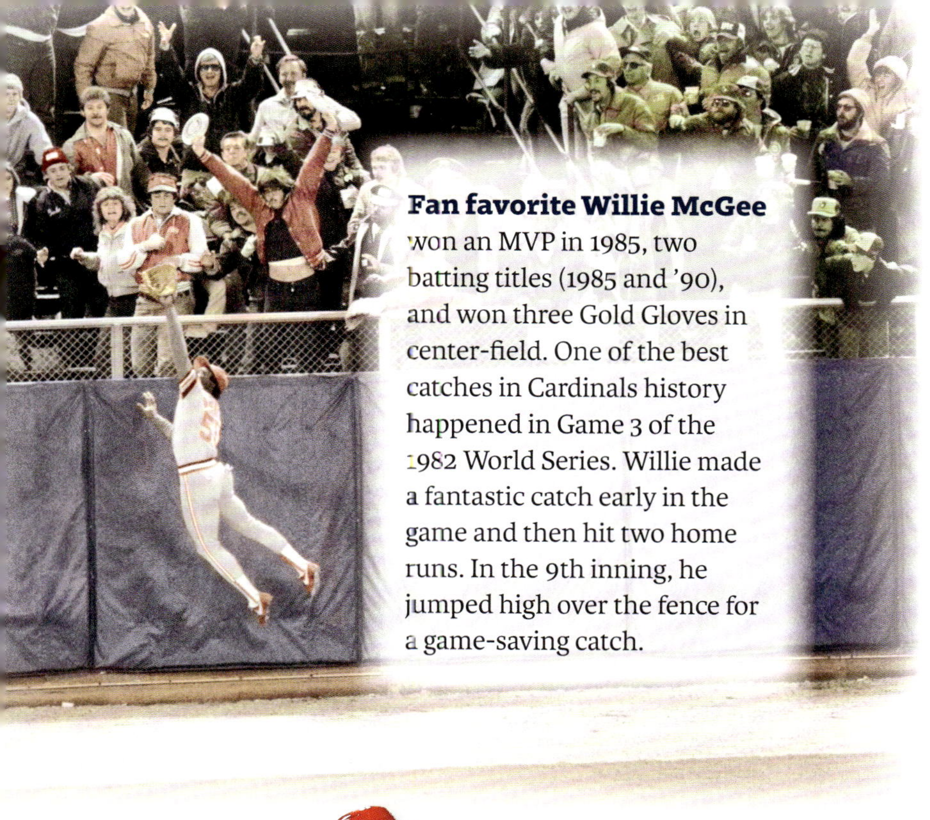

Fan favorite Willie McGee won an MVP in 1985, two batting titles (1985 and '90), and won three Gold Gloves in center-field. One of the best catches in Cardinals history happened in Game 3 of the 1982 World Series. Willie made a fantastic catch early in the game and then hit two home runs. In the 9th inning, he jumped high over the fence for a game-saving catch.

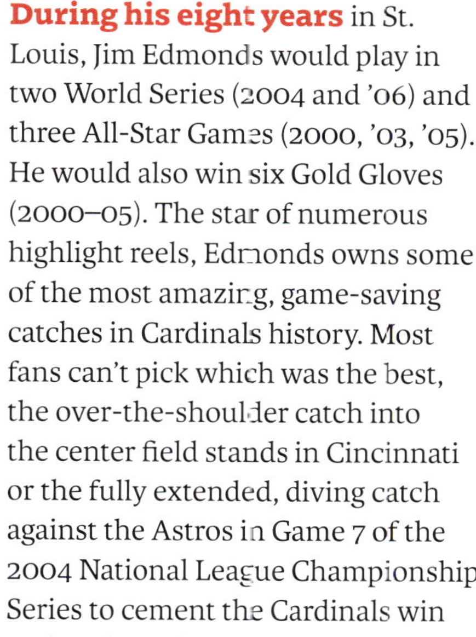

During his eight years in St. Louis, Jim Edmonds would play in two World Series (2004 and '06) and three All-Star Games (2000, '03, '05). He would also win six Gold Gloves (2000–05). The star of numerous highlight reels, Edmonds owns some of the most amazing, game-saving catches in Cardinals history. Most fans can't pick which was the best, the over-the-shoulder catch into the center field stands in Cincinnati or the fully extended, diving catch against the Astros in Game 7 of the 2004 National League Championship Series to cement the Cardinals win and a trip to the World Series.

Matt Holliday came to the Redbirds in 2009. He would be selected to four All-Star games as a Cardinal (2010–12, '15) and played in two World Series (2011, '13). Beginning in 2011, Holliday helped power the Cardinals to four straight NCLS appearances. In 2014, he became only the fifth player ever to accumulate nine consecutive seasons of at least 20 home runs, 75 RBI, 30 doubles, and 80 runs scored.

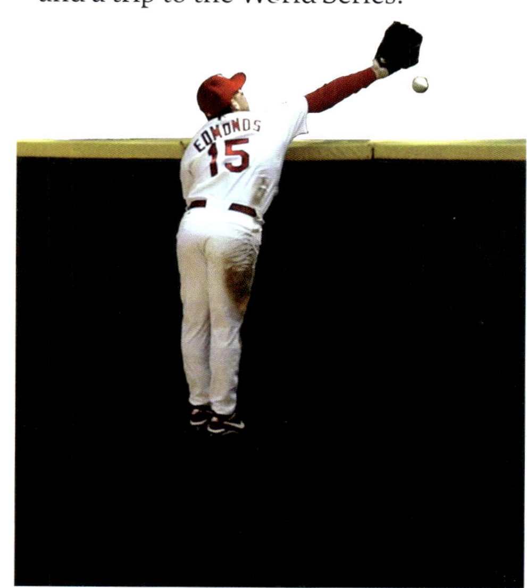

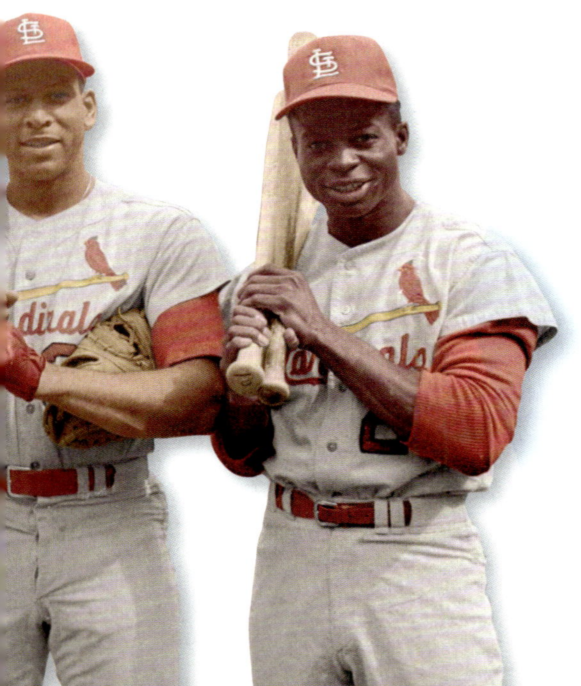

One of the reasons the Cardinals started winning in the 1960s was because they had one of the best outfields in baseball at that time. With Hall of Famer Lou Brock entrenched in left field, they had seven-time Gold Glover Curt Flood in center and one of baseball's best arms in Roger Maris in right field.

These highlighted Cardinal outfielders include four Hall of Famers. As Cardinals they have won five MVPs and were selected to 68 All-Star Games. During their time in St. Louis, they won 10 batting titles, one home run title, four RBI titles, and 14 stolen base titles. All combined, they played on 17 world championships with the Redbirds.

All images on this page credit Getty Images

Catchers

"An on-field Skipper" is what catchers are often called. They have the whole game before them as they set the infield to align to the pitchers next toss. Perhaps that is the reason many catchers wind up being big league managers.

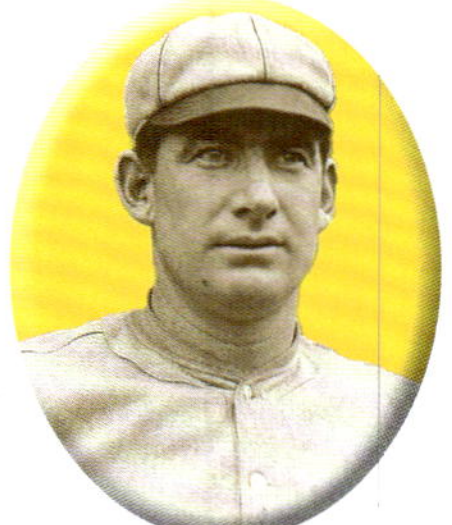

Roger Bresnahan was a playing manager (catcher) with the Cardinals from 1909 to 1912. He was elected to Baseball's Hall of Fame in 1945.

Credit Library of Congress

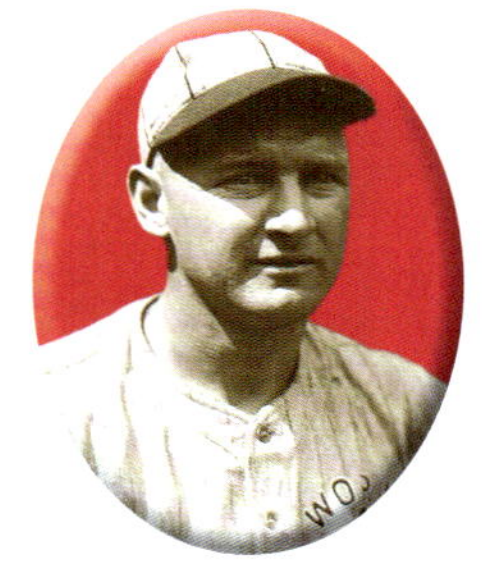

Bob O'Farrell caught for the Cardinals during three different tours with the team (1925–28, '33, and '35). He was the team leader for the two World Series teams of the 1920s and was voted the 1926 N.L. MVP for his efforts in guiding the Redbirds to their first pennant. He became the Cardinals manager when Rogers Hornsby was traded after the 1926 season but lasted just one season.

Credit Getty Images

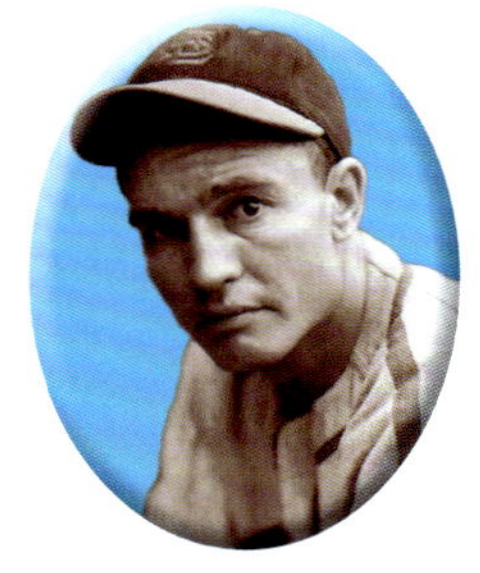

Walker Cooper was the mainstay catcher teaming with his brother Mort in the 1942, '43, and '44 World Series. He was one of the elite catchers in the big leagues during his 18-year career, including eight as a Cardinal. Cooper went to eight All-Star games—three with the Cardinals (1942–44).

Credit Getty Images

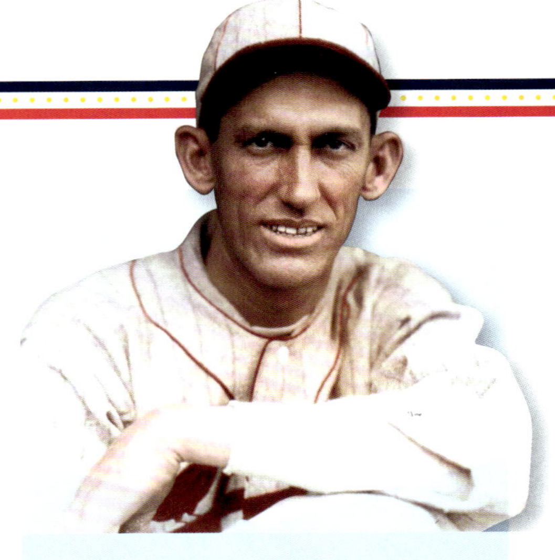

Credit Getty Images

During the 1930s Mike González was one of the first Cubans to play in the Majors, spending three tours with the Redbirds as a catcher (1915–18, '24–25, and '31–32). He then became a longtime Redbird coach (1934–46), which led to two stints as the Cardinals interim manager (1938, '40), making him the first Hispanic manager in major league baseball.

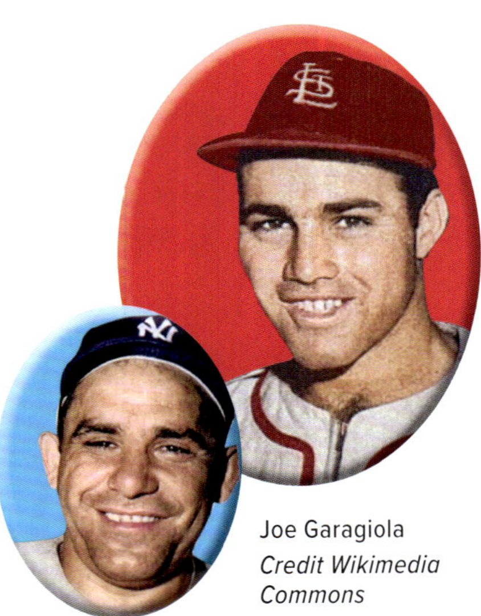

Joe Garagiola

Credit Wikimedia Commons

Yogi Berra

Credit Wikimedia Commons

Joe Garagiola grew up in St. Louis's "Hill" neighborhood across the street from his best friend and future Yankee Hall of Famer Yogi Berra. He debuted with the Cardinals in 1946 and hit .316 in five games of that year's World Series. He stayed with the Redbirds until a mid-season trade in 1951. While Joe was a journeyman catcher playing for four teams over a nine-year career, he soon learned to hit it out of the park as a television host on the *Today* show and commentator on baseball's *Game of the Week*.

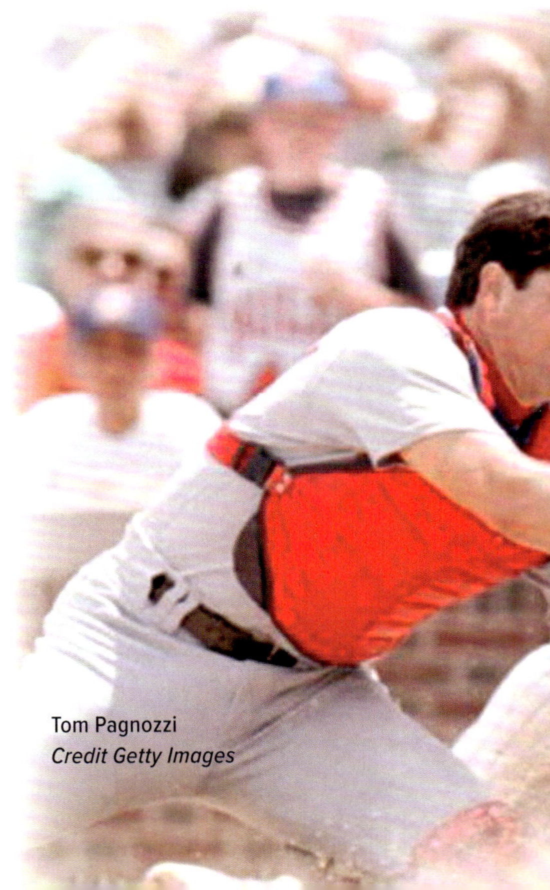

Tom Pagnozzi

Credit Getty Images

Ted Simmons's skills on offense as a Cardinals catcher led him to baseball's Hall of Fame. When he retired, he led all catchers in career hits and doubles and ranked second to Yogi Berra in RBI and second to Carlton Fisk in total bases. He also held the N.L. record for home runs by a switch-hitter. Simmons never made it to a World Series with the Redbirds, but he did play against them in the 1982 Series as a member of the Milwaukee Brewers.

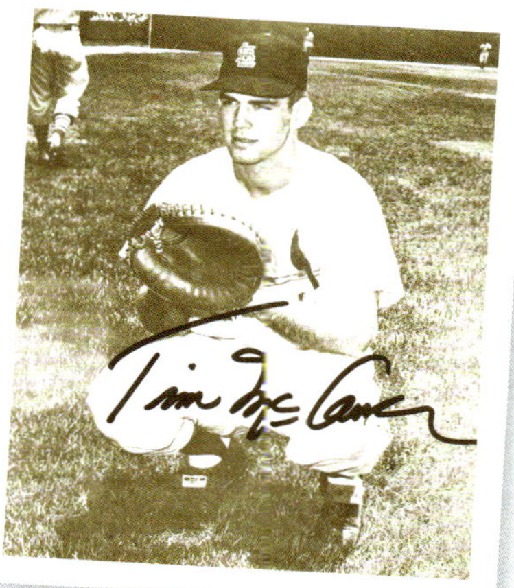

Tim McCarver was behind the plate for the Cardinals' three World Series appearances in the 1960s. A two-time All-Star with the team (1966 and '67), he was one of just a handful of major leaguers to play in four different decades ('50s, '60s, '70s, and '80s) during a 21-year career (12 with the Cardinals).

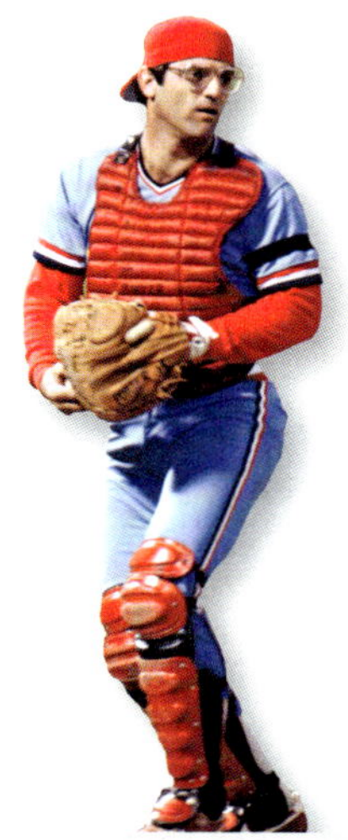

One of Whitey Herzog's first moves in 1981, was to build his new team around Darrell Porter, a power-hitting catcher with great defensive skills who had played for him with the Royals. Porter initially had a tough time winning over Cardinal fans. After signing Porter, Herzog traded away the popular future Hall of Famer Ted Simmons. But Porter showed his value by handling Redbird hurlers and then being selected as the 1982 NLCS and World Series MVP on the way to the Cardinals 1982 Championship.

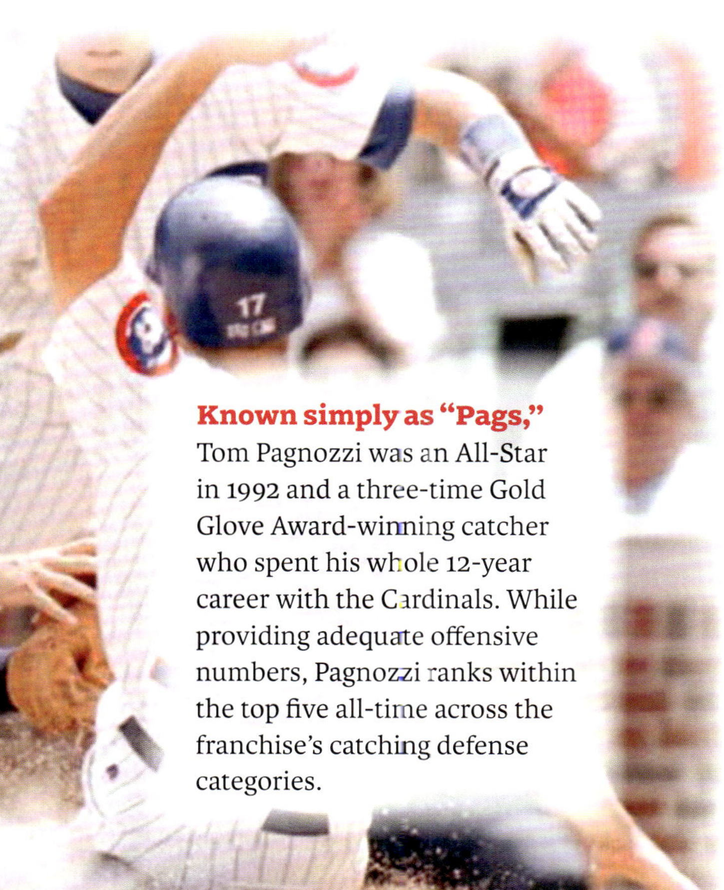

Known simply as "Pags," Tom Pagnozzi was an All-Star in 1992 and a three-time Gold Glove Award-winning catcher who spent his whole 12-year career with the Cardinals. While providing adequate offensive numbers, Pagnozzi ranks within the top five all-time across the franchise's catching defense categories.

Yadier Molina spent his entire 19-year career with the Cardinals. "Yadi" was behind the plate for four World Series appearances and nine other seasons in the playoffs. The future Hall of Famer is considered one of the greatest defensive catchers of all time, not just for blocking pitches in the dirt, but throwing out runners. His list of accomplishments includes 10 All-Star selections, nine Gold Glove Awards, and four Platinum Glove Awards. Molina was clearly a team leader, having gained the respect of coaches, pitchers, and everyone else in the dugout. He also had the respect of all those who played against him. For any player who got on base when Molina was catching, it seemed as though a sign would pop up in their mind: "Warning: Do not steal—Molina's catching." At bat, he became a clutch hitter driving in many key runs at crucial moments. Yadier Molina made himself into one of baseball's best total ballplayers.

All images on this page Credit Getty Images

Managers

The manager is truly the "captain of the ship" when it comes to baseball. With all their success, it's no surprise the Cardinals have had some of the best skippers in the game. It is, however, a surprise to learn the Cardinals' 65 managers over their franchise history are the most of any team in major league baseball.

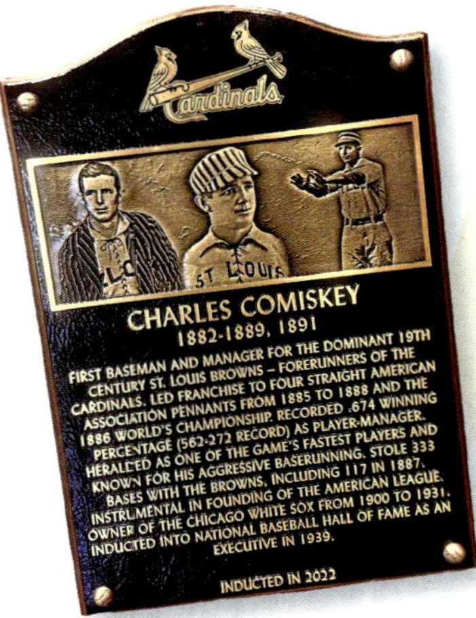

Charles Comiskey managed the great American Association teams that won three consecutive titles while going 562–272 for a .674 winning percentage—the best in franchise history. However, Comiskey is better known in Chicago than St. Louis. In 1901, he helped form the American League and then became the longtime owner of the Chicago White Sox.

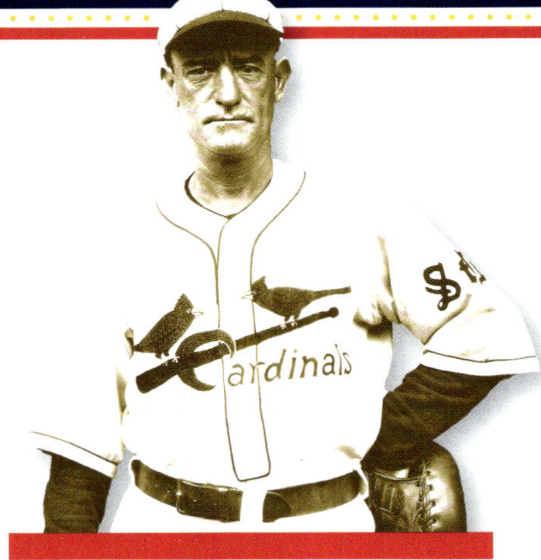

Gabby Street managed the Cardinals to a 312–242 record over parts of four seasons. More importantly, he took the team to back-to-back World Series (1930–31) and won one world championship. Street is probably remembered more for a stunt pulled off the field of play. On August 21, 1908, while he was a catcher for the Washington Senators, Street participated in a stunt to see if he could catch a ball thrown from the top of the Washington Monument (555' high). Street missed the first 12 balls tossed but finally made a clean catch on toss number 13.

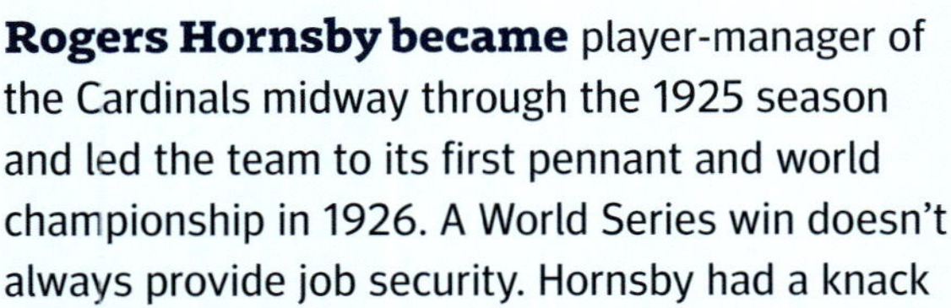

Rogers Hornsby became player-manager of the Cardinals midway through the 1925 season and led the team to its first pennant and world championship in 1926. A World Series win doesn't always provide job security. Hornsby had a knack for not getting along with people—both players and owners. Despite the championship, the Redbirds quickly traded him to the New York Giants after the '26 season for second baseman Frankie Frisch. The grass wasn't greener on the other side, as Hornsby played with and managed three different teams in the five years after leaving the Cardinals. The negative relationships were so bad in 1932 that, after firing Hornsby as manager near mid-season, the Cubs went on to win the pennant and the players didn't vote him a share of the World Series winnings.

Miller Huggins managed the great Yankee teams of the 1920s after getting his start in St. Louis as a player–manager for the Redbirds (1910–17). He guided the team to a third-place finish in 1914, their highest finish since joining the N.L. Huggins became disillusioned after his offer to buy the Cardinals was passed up during the ownership change of 1917, so he left for New York and made history.

Credit Library of Congress

Frankie Frisch began managing the "Gashouse Gang" in 1933 and led them to the 1934 World Series. He compiled a 458–354 record over parts of six seasons.

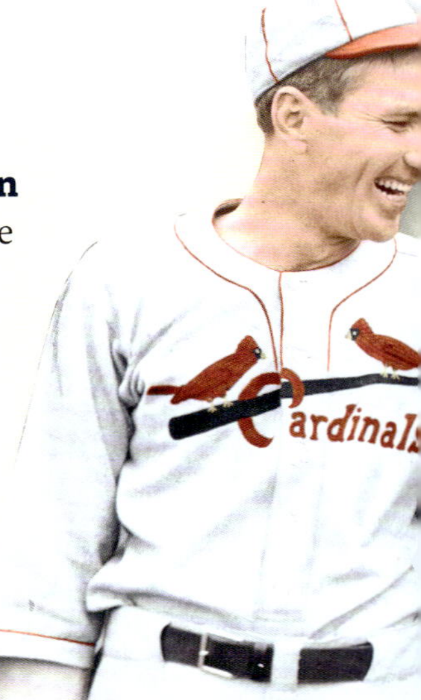

Dizzy Dean, Branch Rickey, and Frankie Frisch
Credit Getty Images

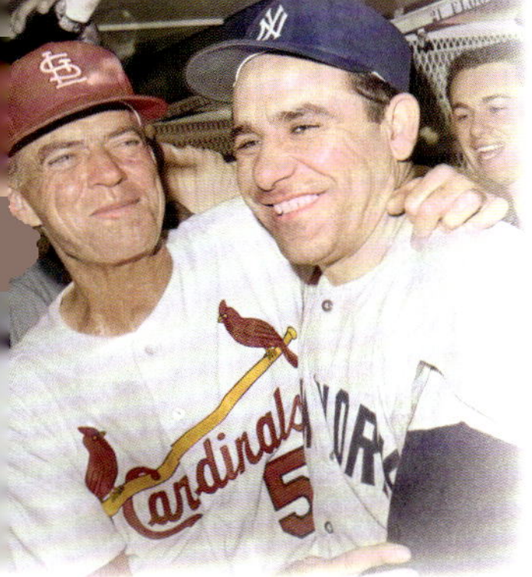

Credit Getty Images

Just like Hornsby learned, winning a Series doesn't necessarily keep you in the manager's chair. Johnny Keane had managed the Redbirds for 2½ seasons prior to winning the World Series in 1964. He left to manage the Yankees in 1965, after Yogi Berra was fired following the Yankees' loss to the Cardinals. Keane's relationship with Cardinals owner August Busch had fallen apart in mid-August 1964, when it looked like the team would not compete for the pennant, and word got out that Busch was set to offer Leo Durocher the job of managing the Cardinals in 1965. Keane got the last laugh by winning the pennant and the Series, and showing Busch what he thought by leaving.

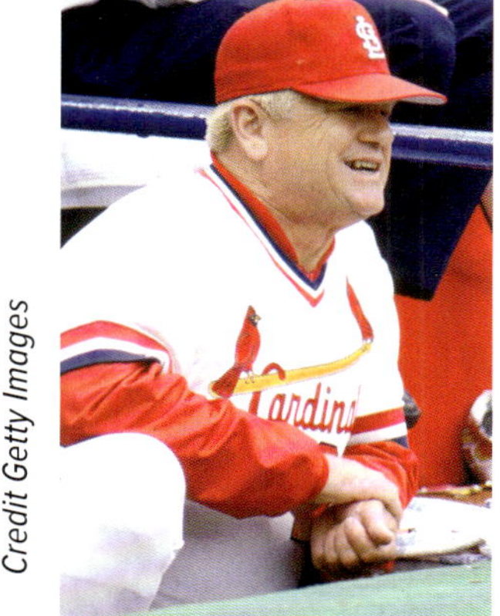

Credit Getty Images

When he came to the Cardinals in 1980 as general manager and manager, Whitey Herzog built a team that would dominate the 1980s. His 822 wins and 728 losses each rank as the third highest within the franchise. Herzog's teams made it to the World Series three times but were only able to win one championship in 1982.

Billy Southworth's 620–346 record includes three straight trips to the World Series (1942–44), and he is one of only two Cardinal skippers to win two championships. His .642 winning percentage leads all Cardinal managers since 1900.

Tony LaRussa became manager of the Cardinals in 1996 and managed the team for 16 seasons. During that period, his teams went to the postseason nine times. They won three pennants, and two world championships. LaRussa and Southworth remain the only two Redbird managers to win two world championships. His 1,408 wins and 1,182 losses are the most in franchise history, and his 2,884 total wins are second most in all of baseball behind Connie Mack's 3,731.

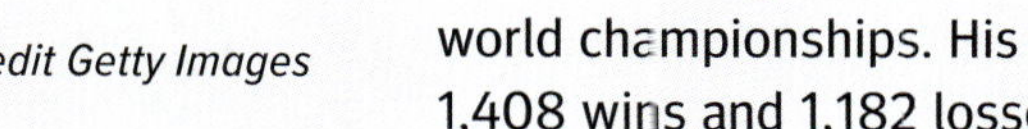

Credit Getty Images

Future Hall of Famer Red Schoendienst took over as manager in 1965 and would manage the team for the next 12 years. His 1,999 games managed, along with his 1,041 wins and 955 losses are the second most in franchise history. Red guided the Redbirds to two consecutive pennants while winning the 1967 World Series.

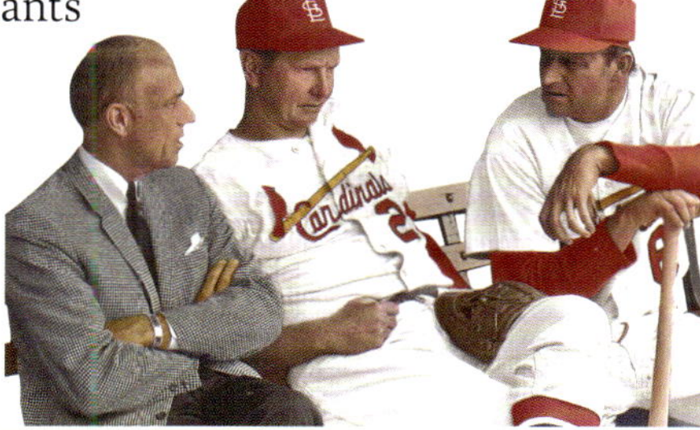

Bing Devine, Red Schoendienst, and Stan Musial

Credit State Historical Society of Missouri

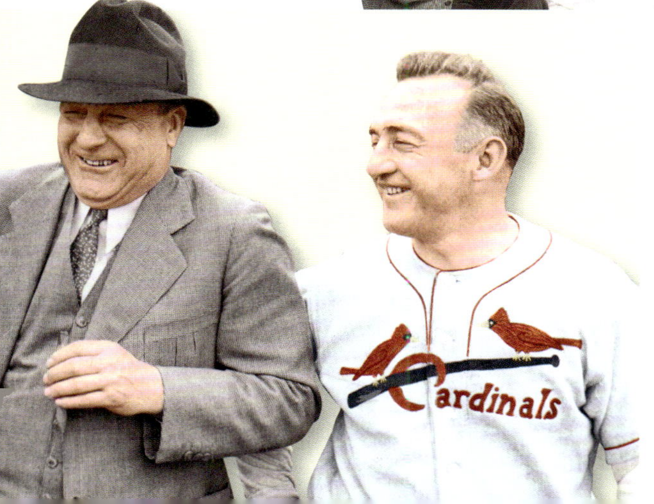

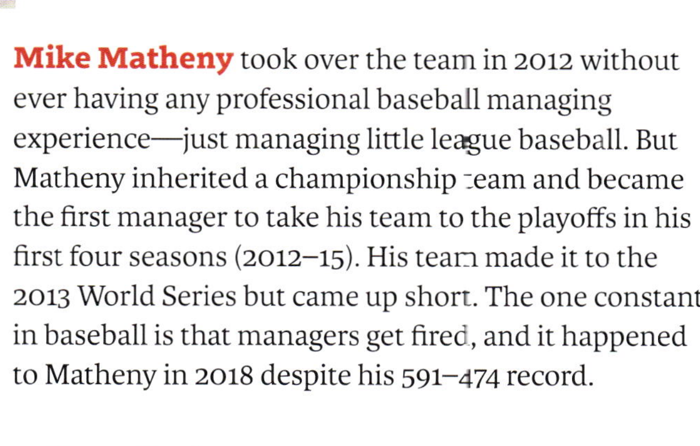

Mike Matheny took over the team in 2012 without ever having any professional baseball managing experience—just managing little league baseball. But Matheny inherited a championship team and became the first manager to take his team to the playoffs in his first four seasons (2012–15). His team made it to the 2013 World Series but came up short. The one constant in baseball is that managers get fired, and it happened to Matheny in 2018 despite his 591–474 record.

Owners and Stadiums

Off the field there is a whole other history of Cardinal baseball from the owners to the stadiums in which the games were played. It is interesting how history repeats itself—even in baseball. It's a history where one beer baron built baseball in St. Louis and another saved it.

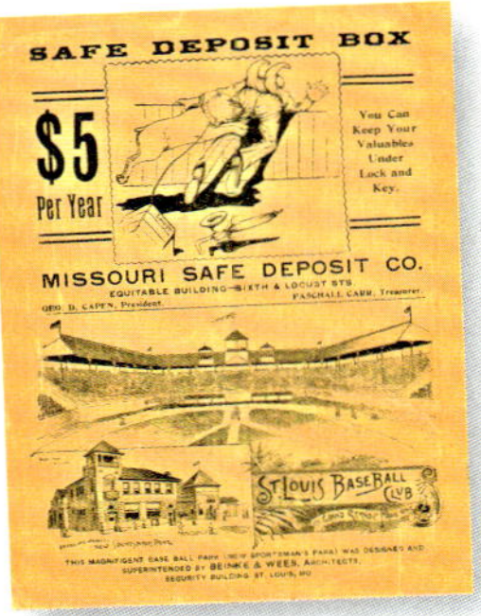

Credit Missouri History Museum, St. Louis

The franchise's first owner was an up-and-coming beer baron of sorts with a bigger-than-life persona. His name was Chris Von der Ahe. The German immigrant knew nothing about baseball but soon realized this sport that was gaining popularity could do good things for him and his beer sales. He bought an independent team and a field, and he eventually took his team from the American Association to the National League. In 1883 he built a new stadium five blocks away from the Sportsman's Park where his team played called "New Sportsman's Park."

In 1899 Von der Ahe sold the team and stadium to brothers Frank and Stanley Robison, who also owned the N.L.'s Cleveland Spiders. They renamed the stadium League Park and changed the team's name to the Perfectos. They then placed the best players from both teams (including Cy Young) on the St. Louis roster, leaving the 1899 Spiders to become the worst team in MLB history (20 wins and 134 losses). Cy Young would get 46 of his 511 big league wins with St. Louis in 1899 and 1900. But Young alone could not make them winners. The team lost 58% of their games between 1899 and 1919 (1,316–1,785).

Credit Wikimedia Commons

After 1902, the Cardinals were no longer the only team in town. In 1901, the American League was formed. A year later the league moved the Milwaukee Brewers to St. Louis to compete against the Cardinals for the attention of what was then the nation's fourth-largest city. The new team would once more take the "Browns" name.

Their biggest losses may have been the deaths of the Robison brothers. Frank died in 1908, and Stanley passed away in 1911. Team ownership then passed to Frank's daughter Helene Robison Britton. "Lady Bee" brought "petticoat rule" to the formerly all-men's club of baseball as the first female owner of a team.

Credit Library of Congress

Unable to offset mounting financial pressures, Britton sold the team to a local consortium in 1917. With the wealth from his automotive dealership, minority owner Sam Breadon established himself as the majority owner in 1920 and spent the next three decades leading the Cardinals to greatness and nine pennants.

Gabby Street and Sam Breadon
Credit Getty Images

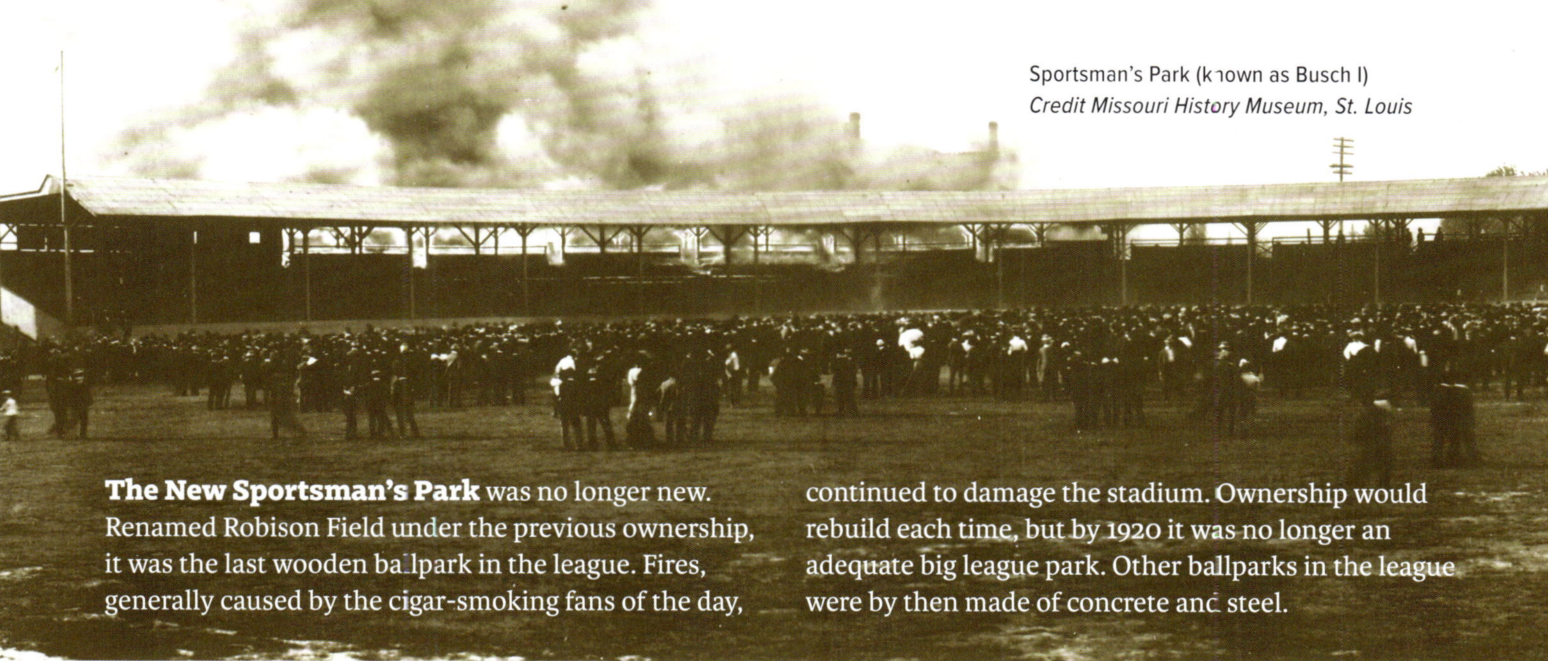

Sportsman's Park (known as Busch I)
Credit Missouri History Museum, St. Louis

The New Sportsman's Park was no longer new. Renamed Robison Field under the previous ownership, it was the last wooden ballpark in the league. Fires, generally caused by the cigar-smoking fans of the day, continued to damage the stadium. Ownership would rebuild each time, but by 1920 it was no longer an adequate big league park. Other ballparks in the league were by then made of concrete and steel.

The team needed a new stadium, but they didn't have the wealth to build one. Would they move to a new city that could provide one? Maybe not! Branch Rickey worked out a deal with his former boss (of the St. Louis Browns) to play in their stadium, Sportsman's Park, when the Browns were on the road. The two teams would maintain that arrangement until the Browns moved to Baltimore after the 1953 season.

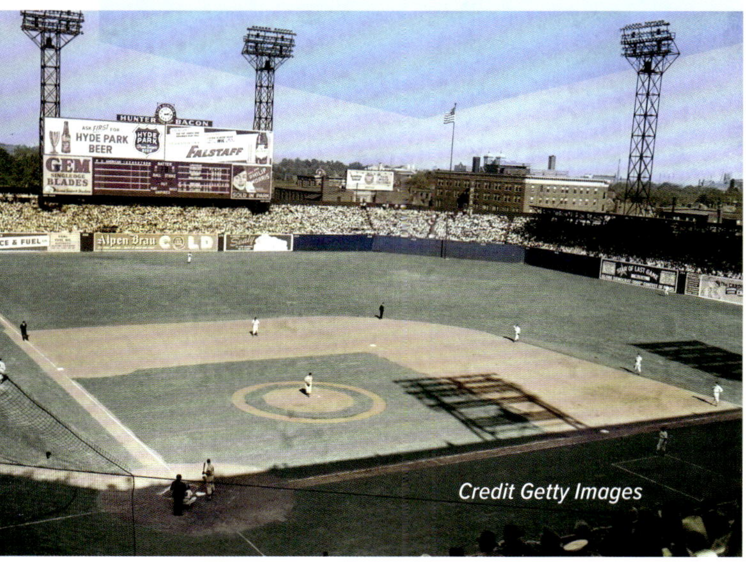

Credit Getty Images

In his desire to win and improve his team, Busch also wanted to improve the fans' experience with a new and upgraded downtown stadium known as Busch II, adjacent to the city's new Gateway Arch. The May 1966 move from Sportsman's Park left behind a historic piece of baseball property that hosted more big league ballgames than any other park in the majors.

August Busch's legacy was six pennants and three world championships. Fans, however, wonder how many more pennants would have been won if Busch had not traded eventual 300-game-winner Steve Carlton over the latter's demand for a $5,000 raise or eventual 220-game-winner Jerry Reuss because Reuss would not shave his mustache?

August Busch passed away in 1989. His son and brewery held on to the team until 1995, when it was sold to a conglomerate of St. Louis businessmen that is today led by Bill DeWitt, Jr. and his son Bill DeWitt III. Not only have the DeWitt's returned Cardinal baseball back to its winning ways, they opened a more modern and updated stadium known as Busch III in 2006. More importantly, since 2000, only the Yankees and Dodgers have won more games than the Cardinals and only the Yankees have appeared in more playoffs than the Redbirds. Proof once more that the Cardinals are the best team in the National League and second best in all of baseball.

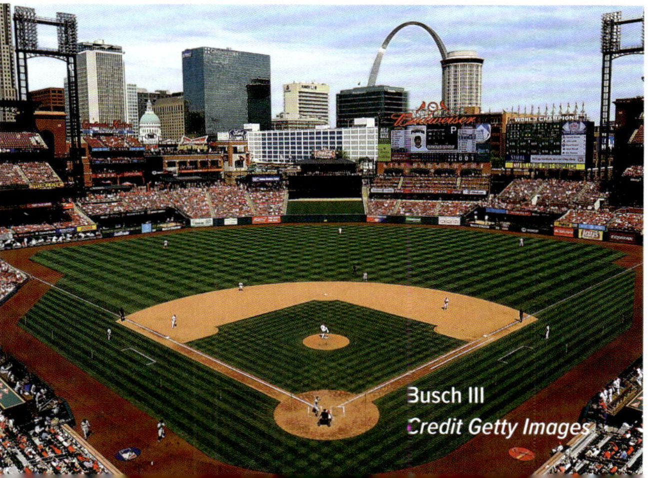

Busch III
Credit Getty Images

Changes to the Game

While the basic game of baseball itself has not changed dramatically since the 1880s, uniforms, gloves, team names, and team colors really have. As described, today's Cardinals have had three different names since they joined the N.L. in 1892. That year the League had 12 teams. In 1901, the League would scale back to eight teams and remain that way until expanding to 10 teams in 1962. Some of the names are recognizable today, but four would eventually change their names: the Beaneaters (Braves), Grooms (Dodgers), Colts (Cubs), and Browns (Cardinals). The Senators and Orioles would move to the American League in 1901, and the Spiders and Colonels would soon cease play.

1892 NATIONAL LEAGUE FINAL STANDINGS

PLACE	TEAMS	WINS	LOSSES	WIN %	GAMES BACK
1	Boston Beaneaters	102	48	0.680	—
2	Cleveland Spiders	93	56	0.624	8.5
3	Brooklyn Grooms	95	59	0.617	9
4	Philadelphia Phillies	87	66	0.569	16.5
5	Cincinnati Reds	82	68	0.547	20
6	Pittsburgh Pirates	80	73	0.523	23.5
7	Chicago Colts	70	76	0.479	30
8	New York Giants	71	80	0.470	31.5
9	Louisville Colonels	63	89	0.414	40
10	Washington Senators	58	93	0.384	44.5
11	St. Louis Browns	56	94	0.373	46
12	Baltimore Orioles	46	101	0.313	54.5

Today many fans believe the Cardinals' uniform is one of the most iconic in all of baseball, yet it has evolved in ways that have gone far beyond changing the name on the jersey. When the St. Louis team began in the American Association, specific colors were assigned to each team. The nicknames of many clubs were inspired by the colors of their socks and uniform trim. In 1882, the St. Louis team took their name based upon the brown stockings they wore with brown piping on their uniforms.

Ice Box Chamberlin
Credit Library of Congress

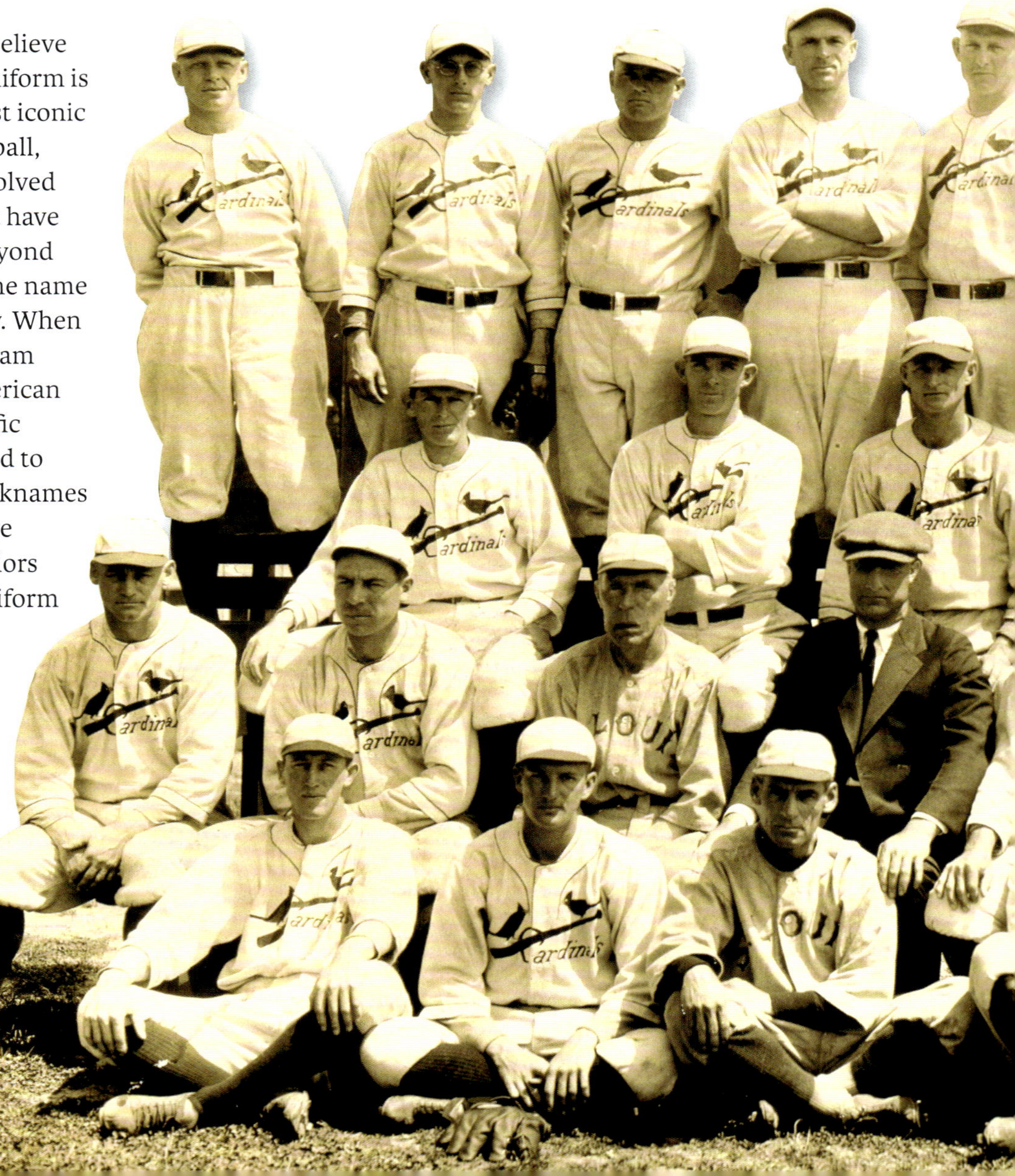

Credit Missouri History Museum, St. Louis

As the team's moniker changed from the Browns to the Perfectos and then to the Cardinals, the coloring of the uniform continued to transition towards today's supporting color of red. But the change didn't come with a logo of the bird until 1922. On February 16, 1921, Branch Rickey attended a meeting of the Men's Fellowship Club at the First Presbyterian Church in Ferguson, Missouri. While Allie Mae Schmidt was decorating the room, she got inspired by two cardinal birds outside the window in the snow and made cut-outs of the birds for decorations. Rickey loved it and had prototypes made that would lead to the birds-on-the-bat logo's debut in 1922.

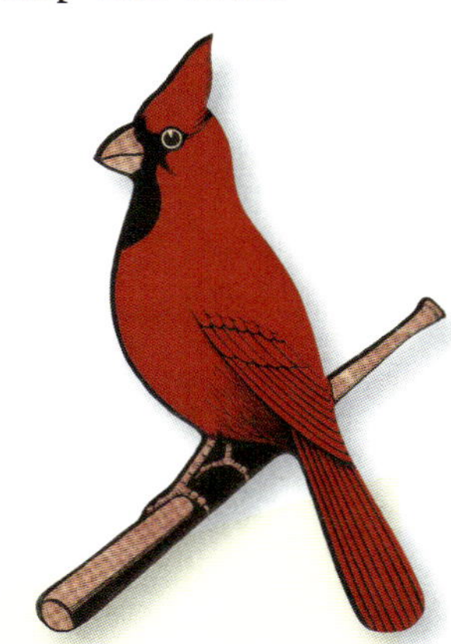

Lane and Manager Fred Hutchinson, Musial in 1956 jersey
Credit Getty Images

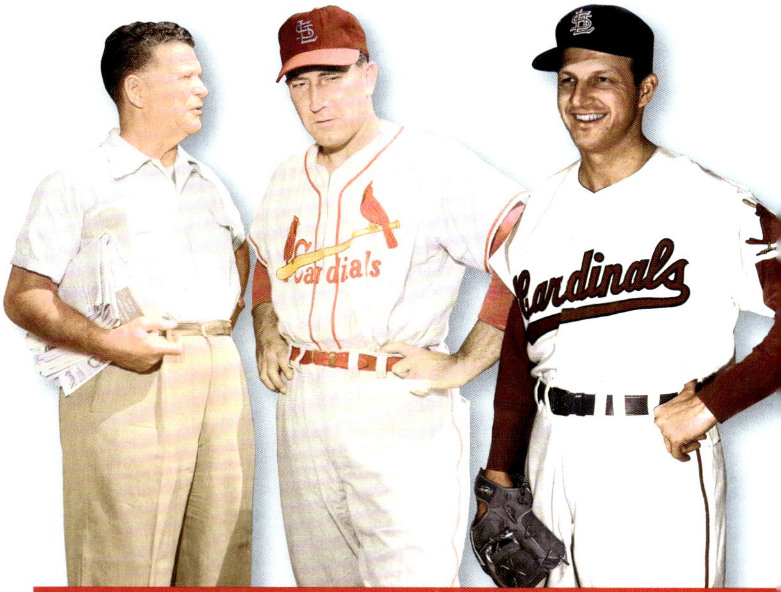

One reason the Cardinals didn't win during the 1950s was their controversial general manager, Frank Lane, who too many times traded away good talent for lesser. But his most controversial "trade" occurred in 1956, when he traded the birds-on-the-bat logo from the front of the team's uniform for the word "Cardinals" in simple, cursive script. Fan dismay ensured that the birds on the bat were back in 1957.

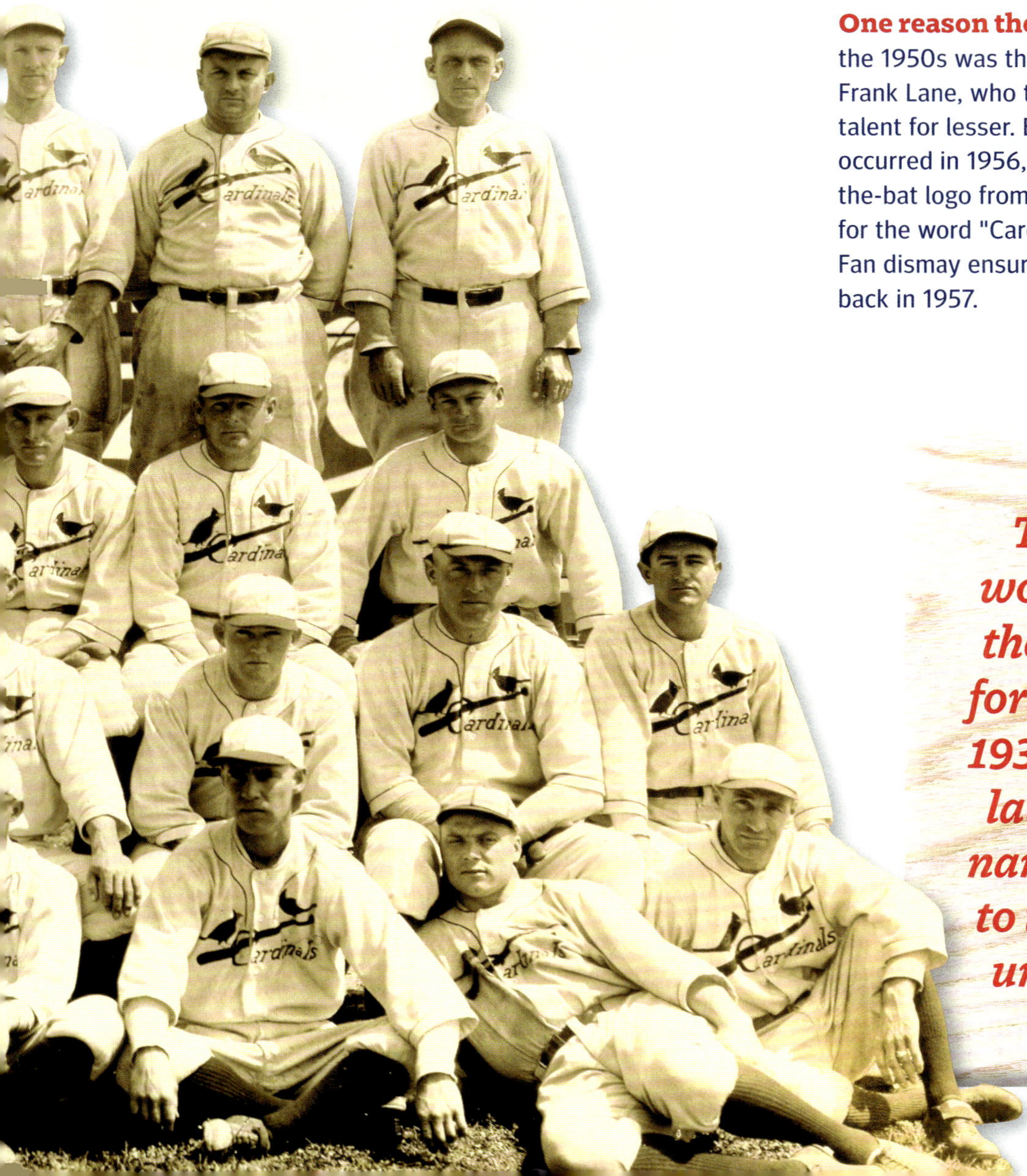

The Cardinals wore numbers on their jersey backs for the first time in 1932, and 30 years later the players' names were added to the backs of the uniform jerseys.

Changes to the Game

Players' hats came in many different shapes and colors during baseball's early days. In fact, there was a different color hat for each of the nine positions played!

Players hats
Credit Library of Congress

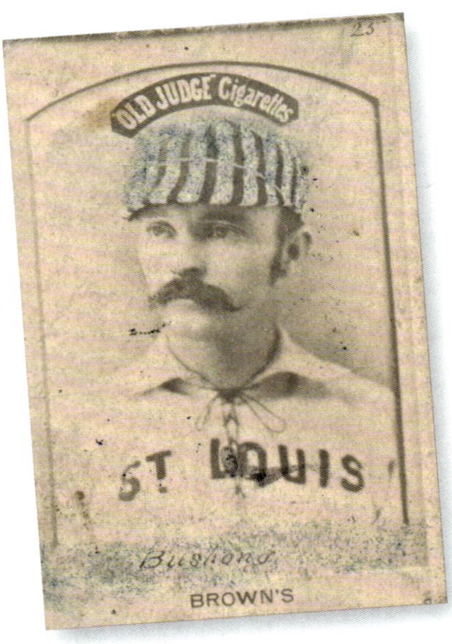

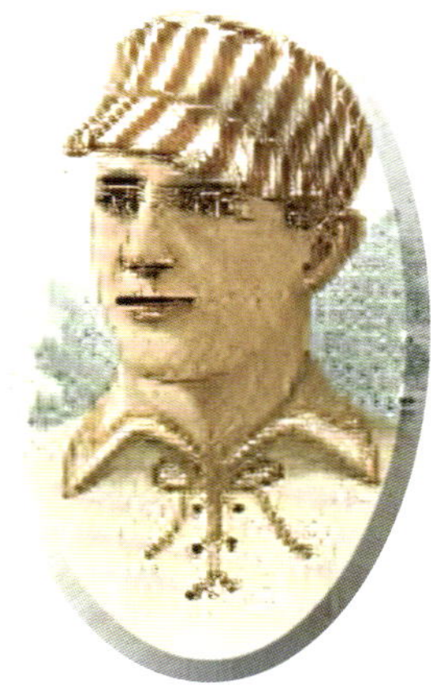

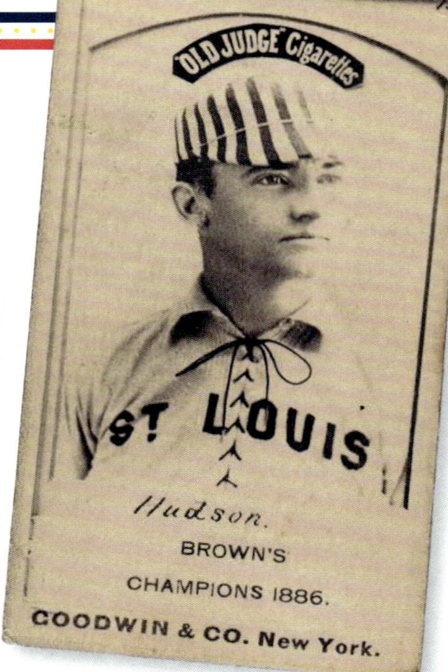

Baseball trading cards have been a staple of the game almost since the game's inception. These early cards provide an insight into the many different versions of hats and uniforms worn over the years.

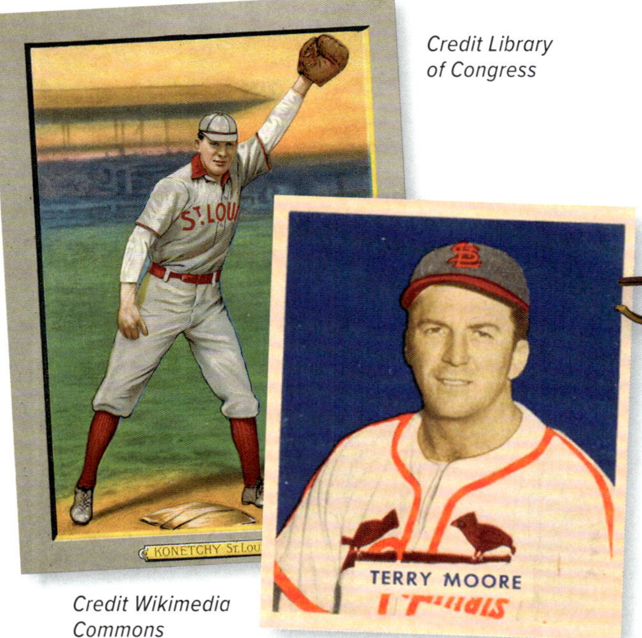

Credit Library of Congress

Credit Wikimedia Commons

Rogers Hornsby model

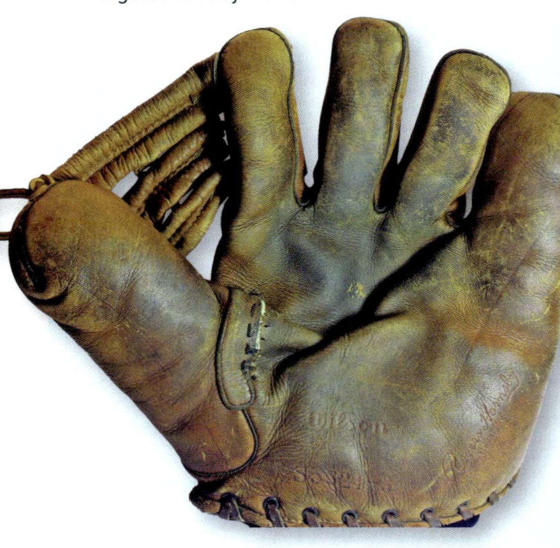

In recent decades the Redbirds have gone from blue hats with red bills, to all-blue hats, and then to all-red hats. They now have a weekend hat and a weekend uniform. In the 1970s they introduced the "victory blue" road uniform that they wore for a decade. One of the most interesting hats of recent times (worn here by Bob Forsch) was the 1976 "pillbox" hat they wore to commemorate the 100th anniversary of the National League.

Credit Getty Images

Marty Marion model

During the golden age of baseball (1950s–1960s), trading cards always came with a rectangular piece of hard, pink gum. Cards collected in the late 1800s and early 1900s, were mostly used as promotions by tobacco companies.

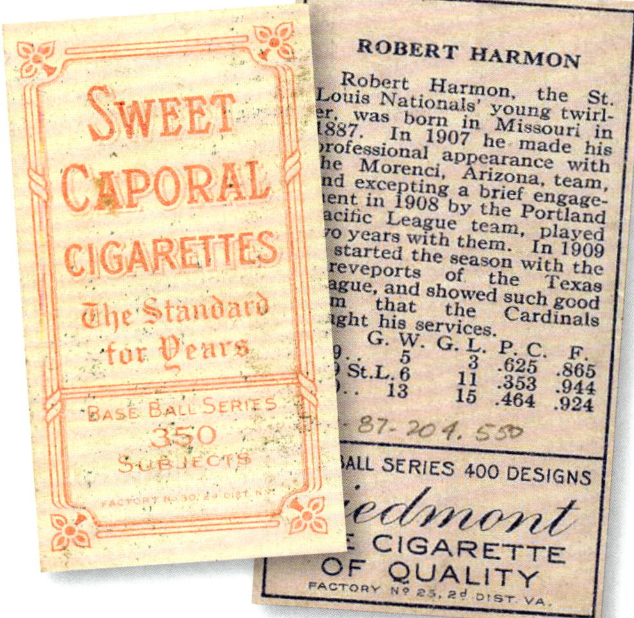

Credit Library of Congress

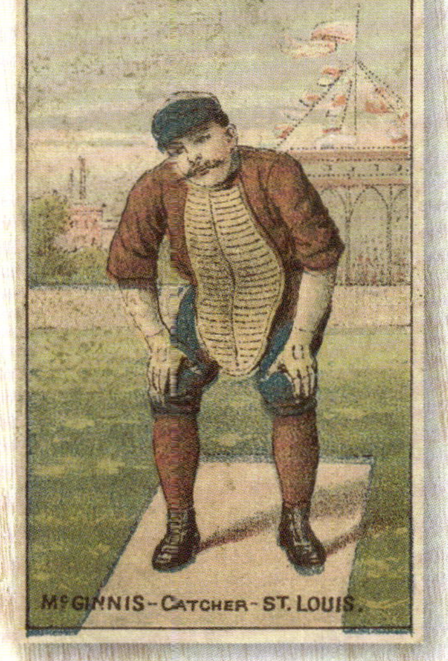

Credit Library of Congress

It is also interesting to look back and see jerseys with laces in lieu of buttons. In later decades, all jerseys had zippers. Often the equipment was different. Catchers, like Jumbo McGinnis that looks nothing like Yadier Molina's, while Browns catcher Tom Dolan is shown wearing a glove on each hand.

There has been a dramatic evolution in gloves as well. There was a reason for the old advice to use two hands when catching a ball. Early gloves like Rogers Hornsby's from the 1920s had no lacing between the fingers to form a pocket. The padded glove simply stopped the ball and the players other hand kept it in the glove. By the 1930s and '40s, the fingers were laced to form pockets as shown on a Marty Marion glove.

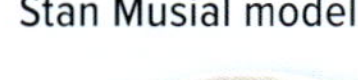

Stan Musial model

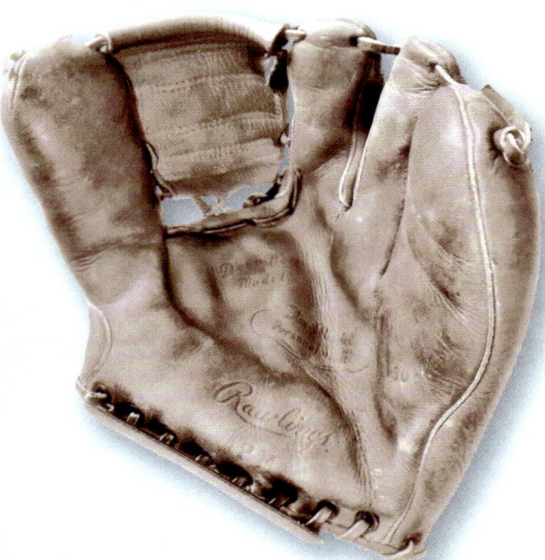

RAWLINGS "BILL DOAK" GLOVES
The One Glove With Which Great Players Make Records
PURCHASED AND USED BY MORE PROFESSIONALS THAN ANY OTHER GLOVE MADE
FINEST CHROME LACE LEATHER EXTRA STRONG
EXTRA LARGE SIZE GLOVE
WELTED SEAMS
SPECIAL METAL EYELETS WILL NOT PULL OUT
LARGE LITTLE FINGER
ADJUSTABLE LACING FEATURE
LIGHT PADDING IN LARGE BALL POCKET
REINFORCED SEAM
READY BROKE FOR USE
EXTRA LARGE SET IN THUMB WELL PADDED
NONE GENUINE WITHOUT Bill Doak NAME
BEWARE OF IMITATIONS NONE GENUINE WITHOUT RAWLINGS TRADE MARK AND BILL DOAK NAME ON STRAP
PATENTED AUG. 22, 1922
EXTRA HEAVY HEEL ASBESTOS FELT HAND MADE
SPECIAL CONSTRUCTED ADJUSTABLE PADDING
MADE OF FINEST QUALITY GLOVOLIUM TREATED CHROME TAN HORSE HIDE EXTRA SELECTED
RAWLINGS Bill Doak GLOVE
PATENTED AUGUST 22, 1922 AND NOVEMBER 21, 1922
ROLL LEATHER BOUND
The Rawlings "Bill Doak" Glove

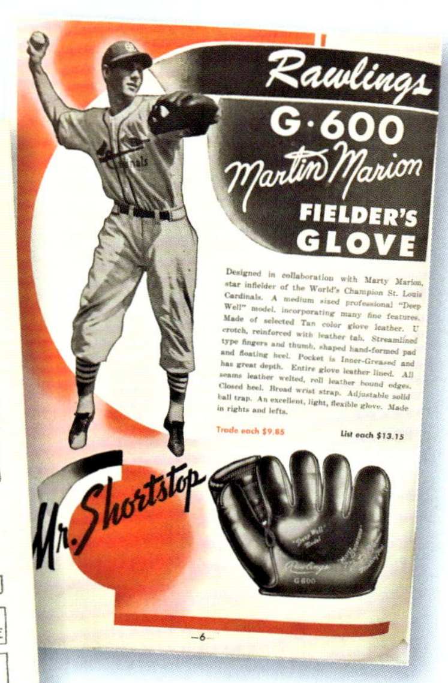
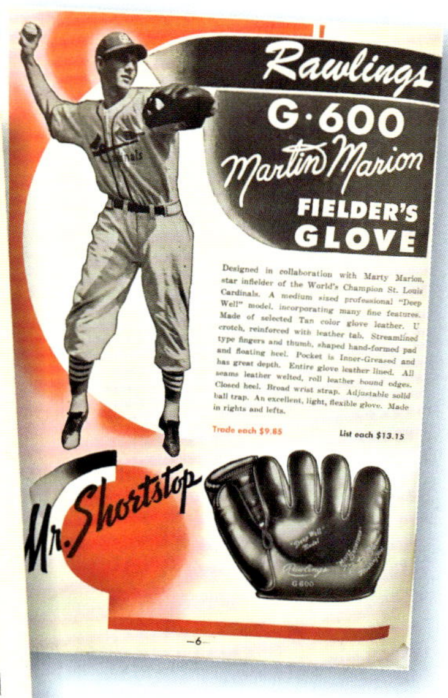

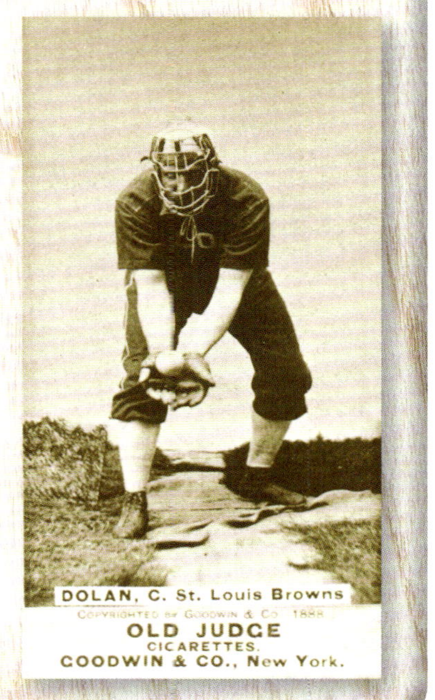

Credit Missouri History Museum, St. Louis

Extra Innings

Special memories are a big part of Cardinals baseball. Many of them were brought to us not at the stadium but in our homes through the voices of Harry Caray, Jack Buck, Mike Shannon, John Rooney, and Dan McLaughlin. They taught us the nuances of the game and kept us on the edge of our seats waiting for the next pitch. For many a child of the 1960s, it is a memory of lying in bed with an earphone attached to your transistor radio, so your mother wouldn't know you were still awake and listening to the game.

Credit Media Museum

Harry Caray's detail calling the game created a picture in your mind as though you were sitting right there in the stands:

"The pitcher toes the rubber, gets the sign, here's the wind-up, the stretch, the pitch!"

When appropriate, you may have heard:

"There she goes, way back, it might be, it could be, it is—a home run!"

Cardinals baseball was so popular that at times, multiple stations would air the games. Today we think of radio station KMOX as the home of the Cardinals. They began broadcasting in 1926, five years after the first radio broadcast of a 1921 game between the Phillies and the Pirates. Owners were initially reluctant to broadcast games for fear that people would not pay to come to the game but instead stay home and listen.

Before there were television and cable TV, radio kept the nation fixated on the St. Louis Cardinals. St. Louis was the most southern and western city in the major leagues prior to 1954. Cardinal radio brought the game to fans listening across these regions and then to St. Louis to watch their heroes play.

Before television, young St. Louis baseball fans could watch Cardinal games for free. Beginning in 1917, the Knot Hole Gang distributed passes to St. Louis school-age children for good grades and behavior as a deterrent to juvenile delinquency. During a time when games started in the late afternoon just as school ended, kids could hop on a street car and soon be sitting in Sportsman's Park watching the Redbirds.

Credit St. Louis Browns Historical Society

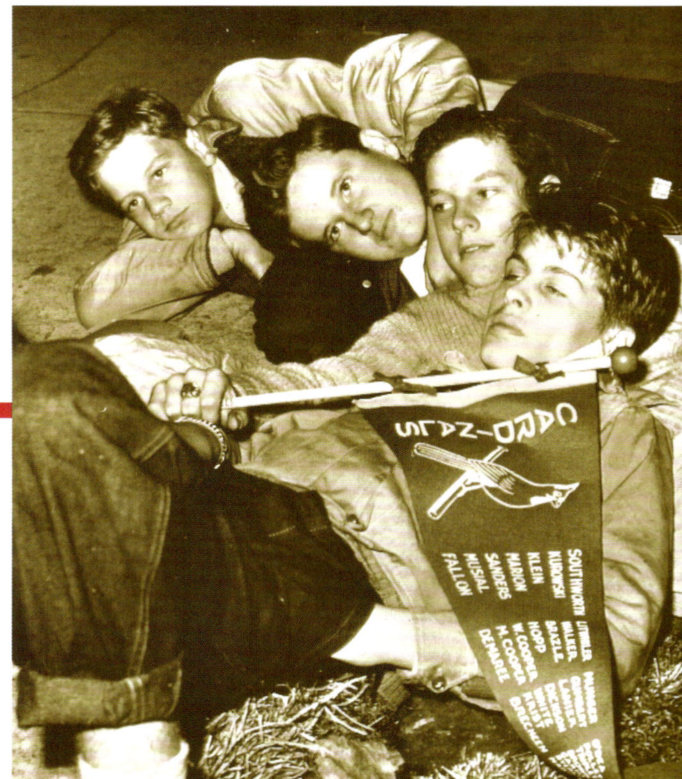

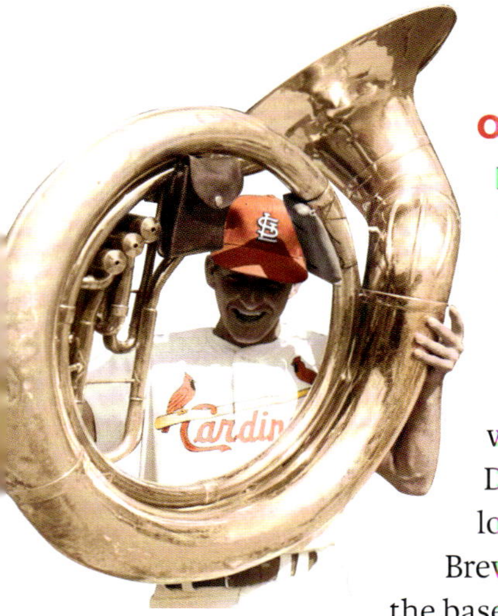

One of the most interesting players in Cardinals history was a backup catcher on the 1964–65 Redbirds. His name was Bob Uecker. Dubbed "Mr. Baseball," Uecker broke up the intensity of baseball with comic relief just like Dizzy Dean and Yogi Berra. A longtime announcer for the Brewers, Uecker also starred in the baseball film *Major League*.

Bob Uecker
Credit Getty Images

Nicknames have always been a part of the game. Chronicled in stories within this book are the more remembered monikers of Cardinal ballplayers. Stan Musial was "the Man," Albert Pujols was "the Machine." The Dean brothers went by "Daffy and Dizzy." Rogers Hornsby had the nickname, "the Rajah" as a play on his first name that was soon expanded to "the Rajah of Swat," as a play on Babe Ruth's "Sultan of Swat" nickname.

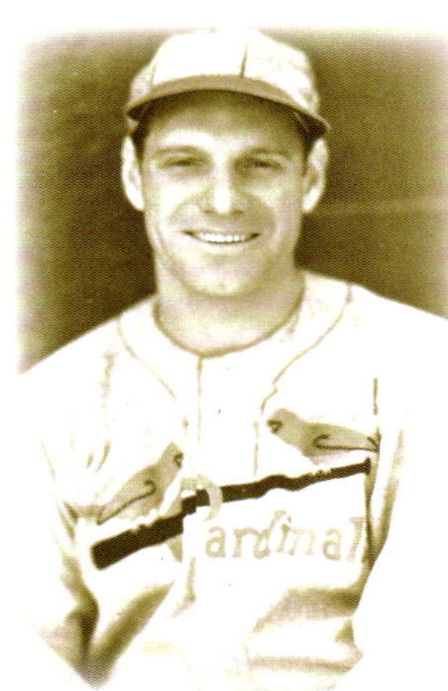

Frankie Frisch was called the Fordham Flash due to his running abilities while playing at Fordham University. Triple Crown winner Joe Medwick actually had three nicknames. He was called "Muscles" due to his physique, but more prominently "Ducky" or even "Ducky Wucky," due to the way he waddled when he walked—something he openly detested. The brash, outspoken member of the "Gashouse Gang," known for saying "nice guys finish last," was Leo "the Lip" Durocher. Bob Gibson's nickname, "Hoot," was simply a reference to former film star Hoot Gibson.

Some of Bob Uecker's best:

"People don't know this, but I helped the Cardinals win the pennant (in 1964). I came down with hepatitis. The trainer injected me with it!"

"The way to catch a knuckleball is to wait until it stops rolling and then pick it up."

"When I came up to bat with three men on and two outs in the ninth, I looked in the other team's dugout and they were already in street clothes!"

Hall of Famer Ted Simmons was called "Simba" as a play on his last name and his long hair, which resembled a lion's mane.

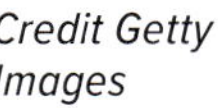

Credit Getty Images

This simplicity and fun of the game could be seen when Dizzy Dean tried playing the sousaphone in the 1934 World Series or when Bob Uecker tried shagging fly balls with a tuba 30 years later in the 1964 World Series. Baseball is a great game, and the Cardinals have had great teams, great players, and most importantly for us all—great memories!

Dizzy Dean
Credit Getty Images

Awards Season

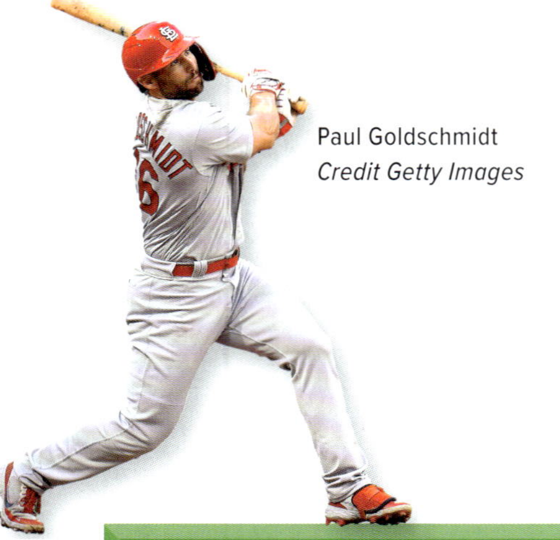

Paul Goldschmidt
Credit Getty Images

The Honor Roll! You don't get to be one of the best in baseball without having the best players and managers. How good were these Cardinals? The accumulation of post-season awards and recognition tell the story.

Best of the Best! Since 1922, the MVP award has been given annually to the season's best all-around player. New York Yankees players have won the award the most (23 times) while Cardinal players are next at 21 selections. Those totals include multiple awards received by the same player. The Cardinals 17 different players winning the award is the most in baseball followed by 14 different Yankee players—a testament to the Cardinals' depth of talent. Which position has won the most MVPs? It's first base for all of baseball and for the Cardinals.

ST. LOUIS CARDINALS MOST VALUABLE PLAYER AWARD WINNERS

YEAR	NAME	POSITION	BATTING STATS				PITCHING STATS			
			BA	HR	RBI	SB	WINS	LOSSES	SAVES	ERA
1925	Rogers Hornsby	2B	0.403	39	143	5				
1926	Bob O'Farrell	Catcher	0.293	7	68	1				
1928	Jim Bottomley	1B	0.325	31	136	10				
1931	Frankie Frisch	2B	0.311	4	82	28				
1934	Dizzy Dean	Pitcher	0.246	2	9	1	30	7	7	2.66
1937	Joe Medwick	Outfield	0.374	31	154	4				
1942	Mort Cooper	Pitcher	0.184	0	7	0	22	7	0	1.78
1943	Stan Musial	1B	0.357	13	81	9				
1944	Marty Marion	SS	0.267	6	63	1				
1946	Stan Musial	1B	0.365	16	103	7				
1948	Stan Musial	1B	0.376	39	131	7				
1964	Ken Boyer	3B	0.295	24	119	3				
1967	Orlando Cepeda	1B	0.325	25	111	11				
1968	Bob Gibson	Pitcher	0.170	0	6	1	22	9	0	1.12
1971	Joe Torre	3B	0.363	24	137	4				
1979	Keith Hernandez*	1B	0.344	11	105	11				
1985	Willie McGee	Outfield	0.353	10	82	56				
2005	Albert Pujols	1B	0.33	41	117	16				
2008	Albert Pujols	1B	0.357	37	116	7				
2009	Albert Pujols	1B	0.327	47	135	16				
2022	Paul Goldschmidt	1B	0.317	35	115	7				

**Tied with Willie Stargell*

ST. LOUIS CARDINALS TRIPLE CROWN WINNERS

YEAR	LEAGUE	PLAYER	TEAM	BA	HR	RBI
1887	AA	Tip O'Neill	STL	.435	14	123
1922	NL	Rogers Hornsby	STL	.401	42	152
1925	NL	Rogers Hornsby	STL	.403	39	143
1937	NL	Joe Medwick	STL	.374	31	154

The Triple Crown is awarded when a player leads a league in batting average, home runs, and runs batted in (RBI). Since 1878, the Triple Crown has only been achieved 17 times in the majors, with Cardinals claiming it three times. Rogers Hornsby (1922 and 1925) and Ted Williams (1942 and 1947) are the only players to achieve it twice. Tip O'Neill won it in the American Association in 1887. Oscar Charleston (1921), Mule Suttles (1926), and Willie Wells (1930) won it while playing for St. Louis teams in the Negro Leagues.

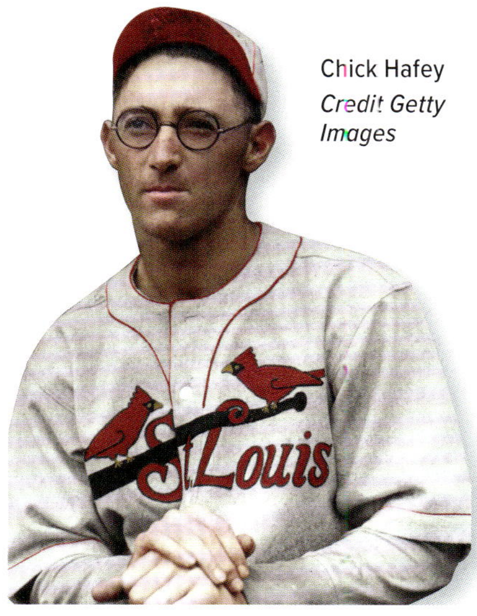

Chick Hafey
Credit Getty Images

ST. LOUIS CARDINALS BATTING TITLES

YEAR	WINNER	AVERAGE	YEAR	WINNER	AVERAGE
1901	Jesse Burkett†	0.376	1947	Harry Walker	0.363
1920	Rogers Hornsby†	0.370	1948	Stan Musial†	0.376
1921	Rogers Hornsby†	0.397	1950	Stan Musial†	0.346
1922	Rogers Hornsby†	0.401	1951	Stan Musial†	0.355
1923	Rogers Hornsby†	0.384	1952	Stan Musial†	0.336
1924	Rogers Hornsby†	0.424	1957	Stan Musial†	0.351
1925	Rogers Hornsby†	0.403	1971	Joe Torre†	0.363
1931	Chick Hafey†	0.349	1979	Keith Hernandez	0.344
1937	Joe Medwick†	0.374	1985	Willie McGee	0.353
1939	Johnny Mize†	0.349	1990	Willie McGee	0.335
1943	Stan Musial†	0.357	2003	Albert Pujols	0.359
1946	Stan Musial†	0.365			

† = Hall of Fame Inductees

Batting Leaders! Since 1892, when St. Louis joined the National League, Cardinal players have won the league's batting title 23 times. Rogers Hornsby won it six times, but Stan Musial did even better, winning it seven times. Willie McGee is the only other Cardinal to lead the league multiple times. The team's eight other winners are a testament to the franchise's overall talent.

ST. LOUIS CARDINALS ROOKIE OF THE YEAR AWARD WINNERS

YEAR	PLAYER	BATTING STATS				PITCHING STATS			
		BA	HR	RBI	SB	WINS	LOSSES	SAVES	ERA
1954	Wally Moon	0.304	12	76	18				
1955	Bill Virdon	0.281	17	68	2				
1985	Vince Coleman	0.267	1	40	110				
1986	Todd Worrell	0.143	0	0	0	9	10	36	2.08
2001	Albert Pujols	0.329	37	130	1				

The Rookie of the Year Award has gone to a Cardinal player six times since it was first handed out in 1947. Not only did these players go on to have great careers in baseball, most were pivotal in their teams' successes.

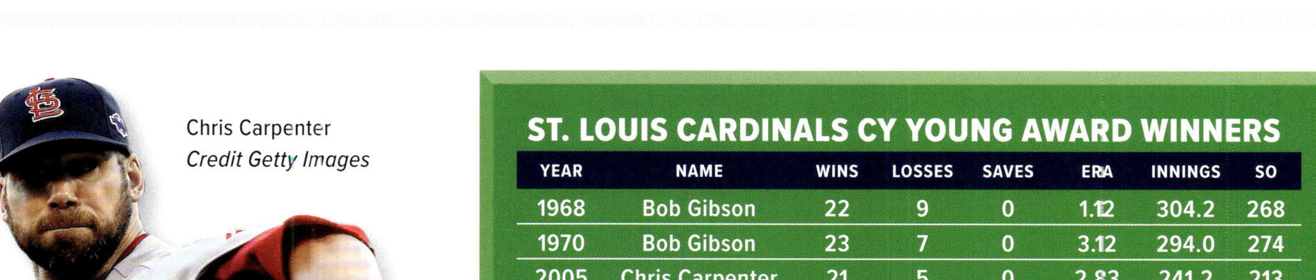

Chris Carpenter
Credit Getty Images

ST. LOUIS CARDINALS CY YOUNG AWARD WINNERS

YEAR	NAME	WINS	LOSSES	SAVES	ERA	INNINGS	SO
1968	Bob Gibson	22	9	0	1.12	304.2	268
1970	Bob Gibson	23	7	0	3.12	294.0	274
2005	Chris Carpenter	21	5	0	2.83	241.2	213

The Cy Young Award was first presented to the best pitcher in baseball in 1956, in honor of Cy Young's passing the year before. Through 1966, it was given to the single best pitcher in baseball across both leagues. Beginning in 1967, each league has given out its own Cy Young award. Cardinal pitchers have received the recognition three times.

Awards Season

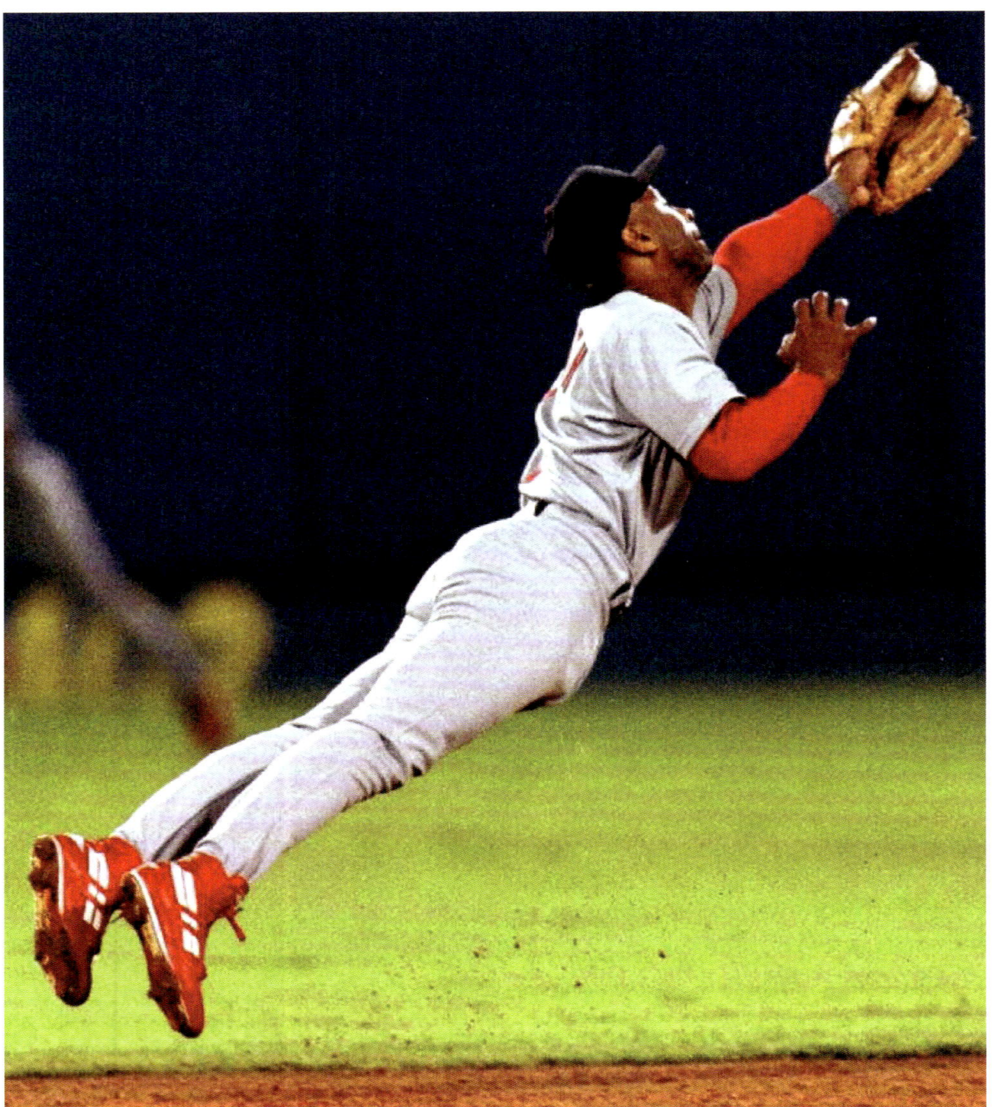

"There's gold in them there hills" was an expression heard long ago during the days of the California Gold Rush. Today gold is found on baseball fields wherever the St. Louis Cardinals are playing. It's in the form of Gold Glove awards given annually to the best defensive player at each position. Good defense makes pitchers better, and there has been no better defense over the years than that of the St. Louis Cardinals.

Ozzie Smith
Credit Getty Images

Since 1957, the Cardinals have won a total of 99 awards through the 2022 season (66 years)—the most by any team in the history of the game. Ozzie Smith is the Redbird leader with 11 wins (he had two additional wins with the Padres). Bob Gibson's and Yadier Molina's nine wins are the second most on the team. Nolan Arenado won two awards with the Cardinals, but he had previously won eight with the Rockies for 10 in a row. That's 10 wins in each of his 10 seasons in the big leagues. How's that for being the best in the game? In 2021, the Cardinals' five winners were more than any other team has ever won in a single year. Multiple teams have won four Gold Gloves in a season, including the Cardinals in 1963, 2002, and 2003—but never five. In 2022, Brendan Donovan was the recipient of the first-ever Gold Glove given to a "Utility Player." Since 2011, the Platinum Glove Award has been given to the best defensive player in each league. Yadier Molina won the N.L.'s inaugural award and three more (2012, 2014–2015). Arenado has won the last two Platinum Awards with the Cardinals to go with the four he won with the Rockies.

ST. LOUIS CARDINALS PLAYERS WHO WON A RAWLINGS GOLD GLOVE SINCE THE AWARD WAS FIRST GIVEN IN 1957

YEAR	PLAYER
1958	Ken Boyer
1959	Ken Boyer
1960	Bill White, Ken Boyer
1961	Bill White, Ken Boyer
1962	Bill White, Bobby Shantz
1963	Bill White, Ken Boyer, Curt Flood, Bobby Shantz
1964	Bill White, Curt Flood, Bobby Shantz
1965	Bill White, Curt Flood, Bob Gibson
1966	Curt Flood, Bob Gibson
1967	Curt Flood, Bob Gibson
1968	Dal Maxvill, Curt Flood, Bob Gibson
1969	Curt Flood, Bob Gibson
1970	Bob Gibson
1971	Bob Gibson
1972	Bob Gibson
1973	Bob Gibson
1975	Ken Rietz
1978	Keith Hernandez
1979	Keith Hernandez
1980	Keith Hernandez
1981	Keith Hernandez
1982	Keith Hernandez, Ozzie Smith
1983	Ozzie Smith, Willie McGee
1984	Ozzie Smith, Joaquin Andujar
1985	Ozzie Smith, Willie McGee
1986	Ozzie Smith, Willie McGee
1987	Ozzie Smith, Terry Pendleton
1988	Ozzie Smith
1989	Ozzie Smith, Terry Pendleton
1990	Ozzie Smith
1991	Ozzie Smith, Tom Pagnozzi
1992	Ozzie Smith, Tom Pagnozzi
1994	Tom Pagnozzi
2000	Jim Edmonds, Mike Matheny
2001	Fernando Vina, Jim Edmonds
2002	Fernando Vina, Edgar Renteria, Scott Rolen, Jim Edmonds
2003	Edgar Renteria, Scott Rolen, Jim Edmonds, Mike Matheny
2004	Scott Rolen, Jim Edmonds, Mike Matheny
2005	Jim Edmonds, Mike Matheny
2006	Albert Pujols, Scott Rolen
2008	Yadier Molina
2009	Yadier Molina, Adam Wainwright
2010	Albert Pujols, Yadier Molina
2011	Yadier Molina
2012	Yadier Molina
2013	Yadier Molina, Adam Wainwright
2014	Yadier Molina
2015	Jason Heyward, Yadier Molina
2018	Yadier Molina
2019	Kolten Wong
2020	Kolten Wong, Tyler O'Neill
2021	Paul Goldschmidt, Tommy Edman, Nolan Arenado, Tyler O'Neill, Harrison Bader
2022	Nolan Arenado, Brendan Donovan

Won the National League Pennant | *In the Playoffs*

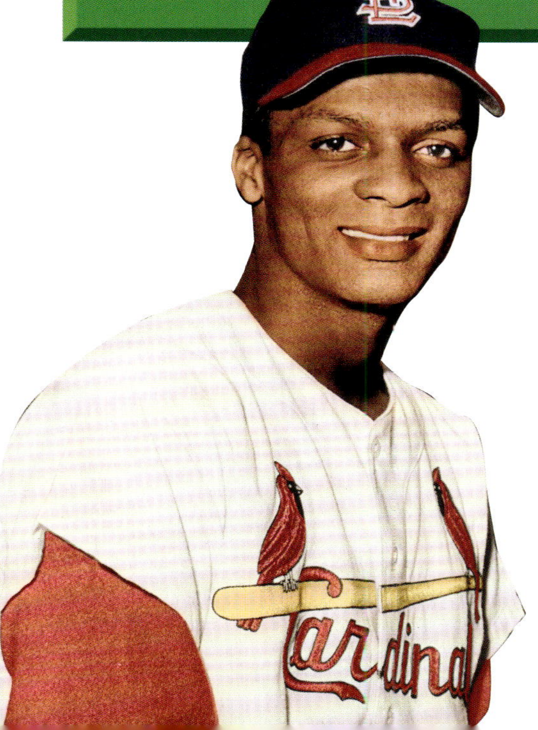

Curt Flood
Credit Missouri History Museum, St. Louis

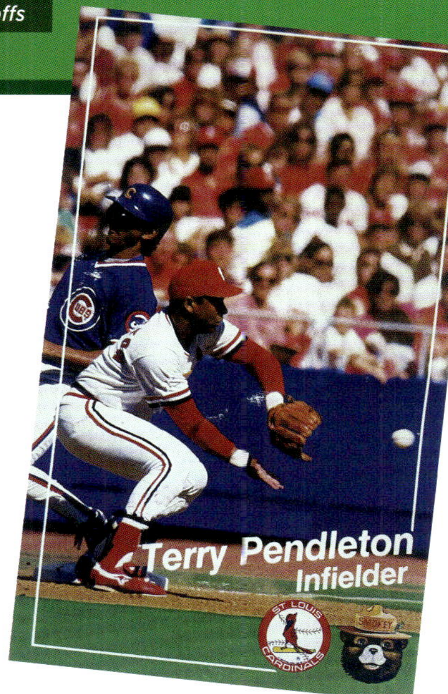

Awards Season

The St. Louis Cardinals Hall of Fame! While the National Baseball Hall of Fame honors the best of the best in all of baseball, the local St. Louis Cardinals Hall of Fame was established in 2014 by the team to honor those great players, managers, coaches, executives, and announcers who made the Cardinals franchise one of the best in baseball. While many will never be called to Cooperstown, their contributions stand out and are now recognized with their plaques included in the St. Louis Cardinals Hall of Fame Museum located in Ballpark Village outside Busch Stadium.

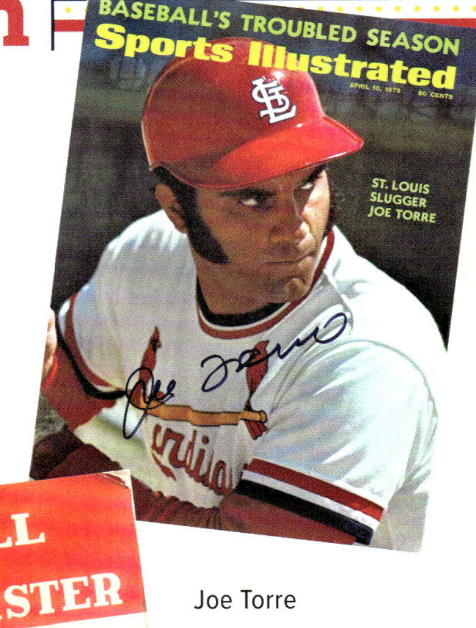

Joe Torre

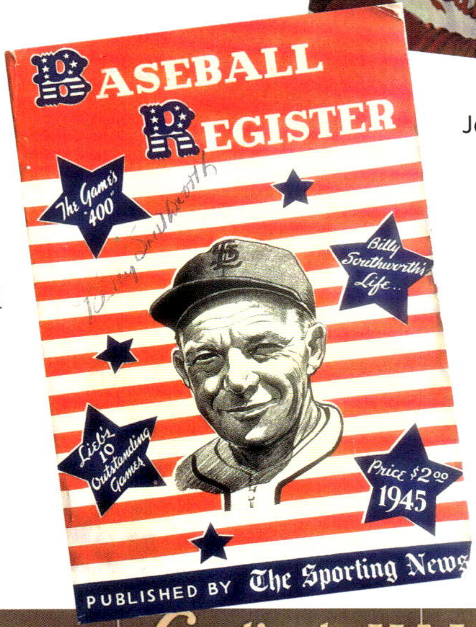

Billy Southworth

Cardinals in Cooperstown! Fifty three men associated with the Brown Stockings, Browns, Perfectos, and Cardinals teams of this franchise have been inducted into the National Baseball Hall of Fame in Cooperstown, New York. These inductions include players, managers, and executives. Some only played a few seasons with the franchise, while others spent their whole career in the Gateway City. Of these 54 individuals, 18 have been inducted as Cardinals, but each and every man listed had a part of their career with the team.

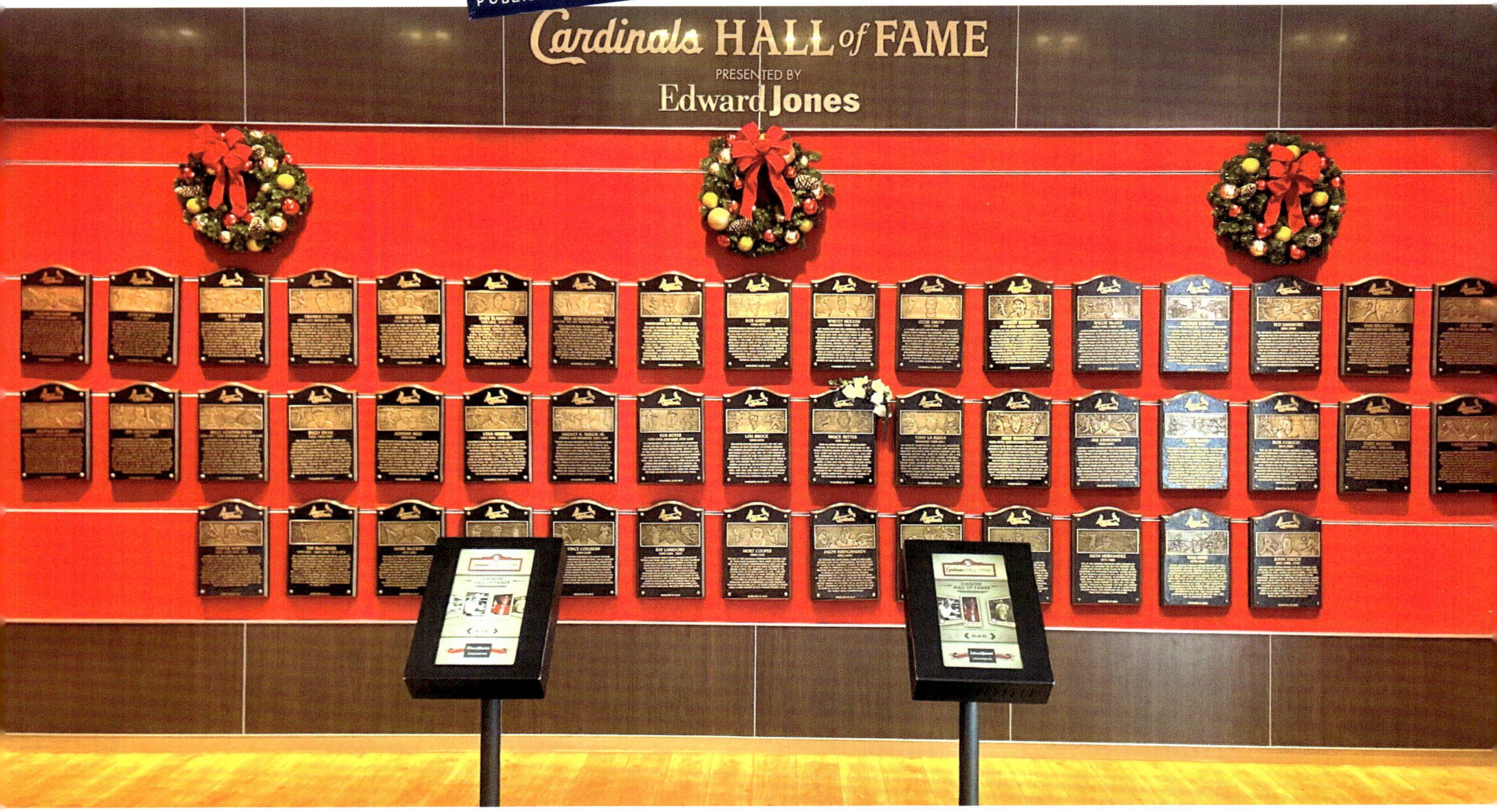

BASEBALL HALL OF FAME INDUCTEES WHO PLAYED FOR THE ST. LOUIS FRANCHISE

PLAYERS	YEARS AS CARDINAL	ROLE(S)	YEAR INDUCTED
Grover Cleveland Alexander	1926–1929	Player	1938
Walter Alston	1936	Manager	1983
Jake Beckley	1904–1907	Player	1971
Jim Bottomley*	1922–1932	Player	1974
Roger Bresnahan	1909–1912	Player	1945
Lou Brock*	1964–1979	Player	1985
Mordecai Brown	1903	Player	1949
Jesse Burkett	1899–1901	Player	1946
Steve Carlton	1965–1971	Player	1994
Orlando Cepeda	1966–1968	Player	1999
Charles Comiskey	1882–1889 1891	Pioneer/ Executive	1939
Roger Connor	1894–1897	Player	1976
Dizzy Dean*	1930 1932–1937	Player	1953
Leo Durocher*	1933–1937	Manager	1994
Dennis Eckersley	1996–1997	Player	2004
Frankie Frisch*	1927–1938	Player	1947
Pud Galvin	1875, 1892	Player	1965
Bob Gibson*	1959–1975	Player	1981
Clark Griffith	1891	Player	1946
Burleigh Grimes	1930–1934	Player	1964
Chick Hafey*	1924–1931	Player	1971
Jesse Haines*	1920–1937	Player	1970
Whitey Herzog	1980–1990	Manager	2010
Rogers Hornsby*	1915–1926 1933	Player	1942
Miller Huggins	1910–1917	Manager	1964
Jim Kaat	1980–1983	Player	2022
Tony LaRussa	1996–2011	Manager	2014
Rabbit Maranville	1927–1928	Player	1954
Tommy McCarthy	1888–1891	Player	1946
John McGraw	1900	Manager	1937
Bill McKechnie	1928–1929	Manager	1962
Joe Medwick*	1932–1940 1947–1948	Player	1968
Minnie Miñoso	1962	Player	2022
Johnny Mize*	1936–1941	Player	1981
Stan Musial*	1941–1944 1946–1963	Player	1969
Kid Nichols	1904–1905	Player	1949
Branch Rickey	1919–1942	Pioneer/ Executive	1967
Wilbert Robinson	1900	Manager	1946
Scott Rolen	2002–2007	Player	2023
Red Schoendienst*	1945–1956 1961–1976 1979–1995	Player	1989
Enos Slaughter*	1938–1942 1946–1953	Player	1985
Lee Smith	1990–1993	Player	2019
Ozzie Smith*	1982–1999	Player	2002
John Smoltz	2009	Player	2015
Billy Southworth	1926–1927 1929 1940–1945	Manager	2008
Bruce Sutter	1981–1984	Player	2006
Joe Torre	1969–1974 1990–1995	Manager	2014
Dazzy Vance	1933–1934	Player	1955
Larry Walker	2004–2005	Player	2020
Bobby Wallace	1899–1901 1917–1918	Player	1953
Hoyt Wilhelm	1957	Player	1985
Vic Willis	1910	Player	1995
Cy Young	1899–1900	Player	1937

**Played more games with Cardinals than any other team*

Inducted as a St. Louis Cardinal

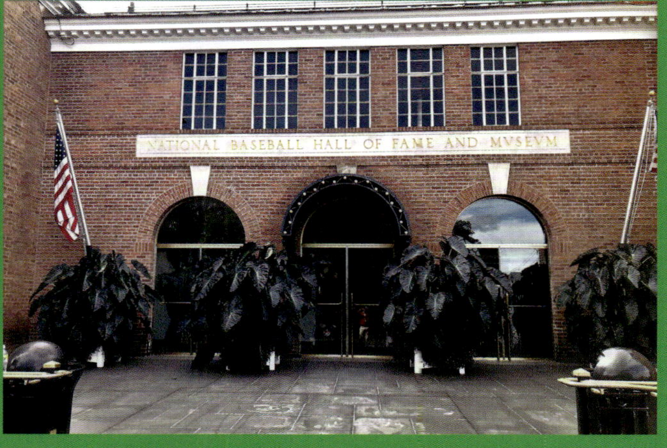

Index

1911 St. Louis Cardinals
Credit Library of Congress

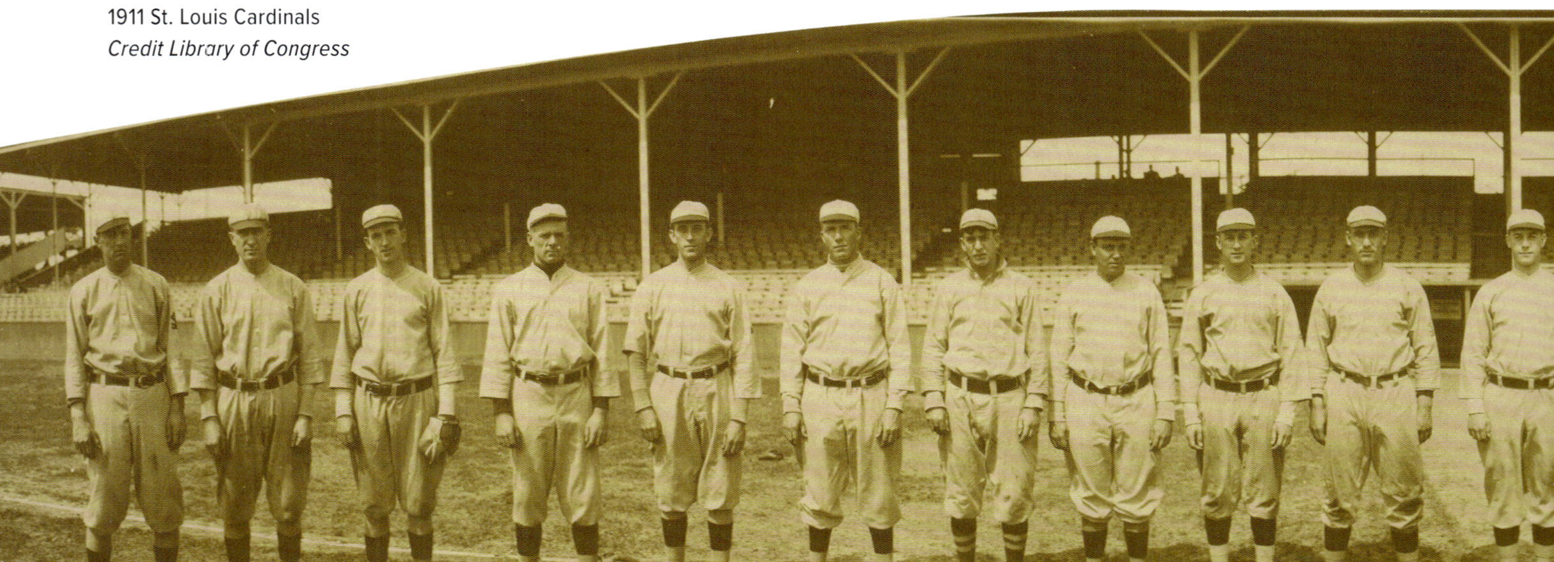

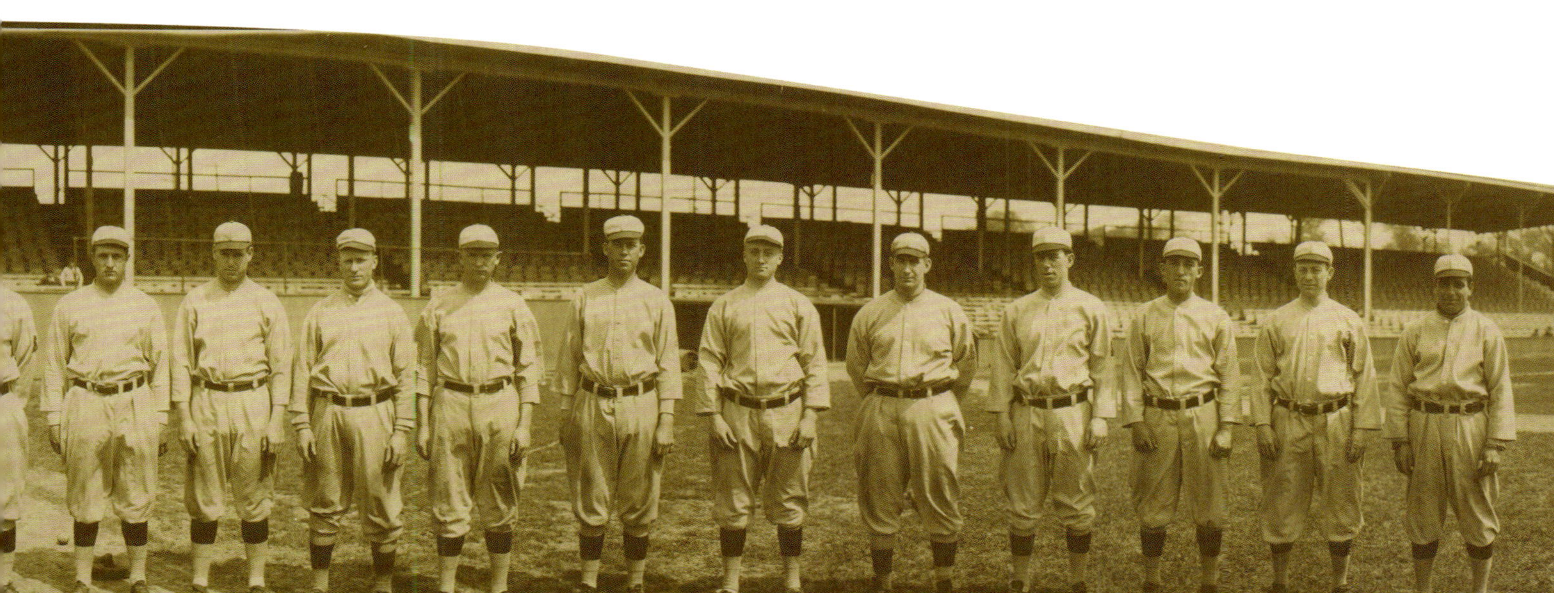

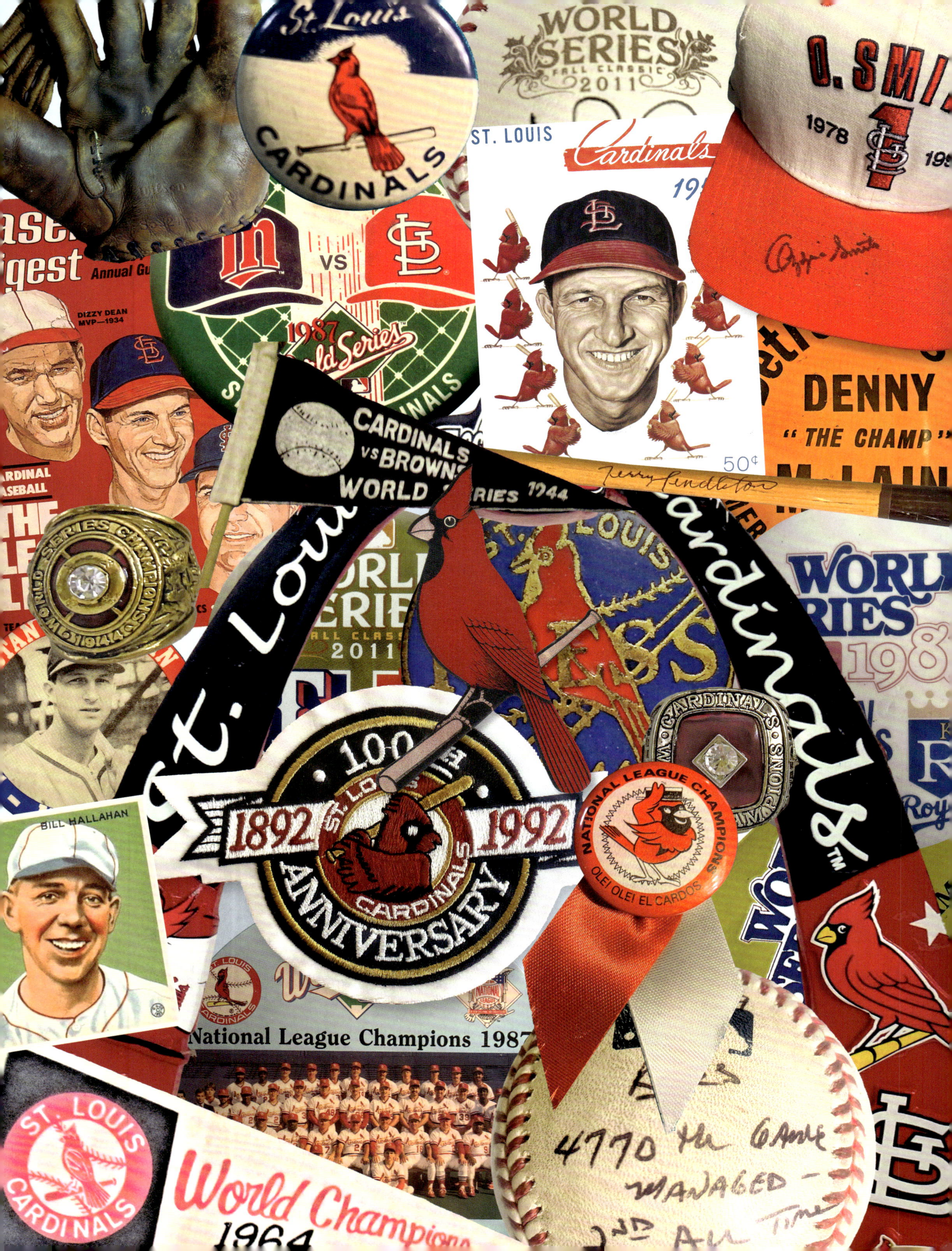
St. Louis
CARDINALS
WORLD SERIES
FALL CLASSIC
2011
1978
ST. LOUIS
Cardinals
VS
1987
World Series
DIZZY DEAN
MVP—1934
DENNY
"THE CHAMP"
50¢
CARDINALS
vs BROWNS
WORLD
1944
St. Louis Cardinals
BILL HALLAHAN
100
1892
1992
CARDINALS
ANNIVERSARY
NATIONAL LEAGUE CHAMPIONS
OLE! OLE! EL CARDOS
CARDINALS
National League Champions 1987
ST. LOUIS
CARDINALS
World Champions
1964
4770 the GAME
MANAGED -